OUTSOURCING HUMAN RESOURCES FUNCTIONS

Second Edition

OUTSOURCING HUMAN RESOURCES FUNCTIONS

HOW, WHY, WHEN, AND WHEN NOT TO
CONTRACT FOR HR SERVICES

MARY F. COOK and SCOTT B. GILDNER

Society for Human Resource Management
Alexandria, Virginia
USA
www.shrm.org

The Society for Human Resource Management (SHRM) is the world's largest association devoted to human resource management. Representing more than 200,000 individual members, the Society serves the needs of HR professionals by providing the most essential and comprehensive set of resources available. As an influential voice, SHRM is committed to advancing the human resource profession to ensure that HR is an essential and effective partner in developing and executing organizational strategy. Visit SHRM Online at www.shrm.org.

Library of Congress Cataloging-in-Publication Data

Cook, Mary F., 1937-
 Outsourcing human resources functions : how, why, when, and when not to contract for HR services / Mary F. Cook and Scott R. Gildner.-- 2nd ed.
     p. cm.
 Includes index.
 ISBN 1-58644-068-3
 1. Personnel management--United States. 2. Contracting out--United States. I. Gildner, Scott R. II. Title.

HF5549.2.U5C664 2006
658.300973--dc22

                              2006005455

Edited by: Publications Professionals LLC
Index by: Sharon Johnson
Cover design by: Matthew Hlubny
Interior design and layout by: Matthew Hlubny
Printed by: Central Plains Book Manufacturing

Printed in the United States of America.
10 9 8 7 6 5 4 3 2 1

Contents

CD-ROM Contents

Abbreviations and Acronyms Used in HR Outsourcing
Glossary of Human Resource and Outsourcing Terms
Sample Request for Information (RIF)
Sample Overview to a Request for Proposals (RFP)
Sample Administrative Services Agreement
Sample Consulting Services Agreement

Figures and Tables

Preface

No other business strategy has had more overall effect on organizations today than outsourcing. Literally hundreds of thousands of companies, large and small, are in the process of outsourcing a variety of business functions, including human resource (HR) management.

No organization can stay competitive in today's environment by relying solely on its own resources. Today's global economy forces executives to reexamine every aspect of their business against a single standard-"best in the world." So how do executives find the speed, flexibility, and scalability needed to overcome the challenges of today's turbulent business world? Through outsourcing.

Whether you think this strategy is a good one or not, if you are in business, this process will be one that you will use at some point in your career. The question is no longer whether organizations will embrace outsourcing, but rather when they will turn to this solution for many of their internal staff functions.

Outsourcing has become an integral part of the corporate landscape, and human resources is responsible for its implementation in most organizations. This trend suggests a dynamic environment for human resources over the next ten years, and HR professionals who grasp the significance of this transformation will enjoy unparalleled career opportunities.

This book, *Outsourcing Human Resources Functions, Second Edition*, provides a roadmap and is a quick-reference guide for HR executives, as well as chief executive officers and chief operating officers who have ventured into the world of outsourcing or who are contemplating doing so. Outsourcing is not a process to enter into lightly. It can reduce costs, it can provide an avenue for acquiring needed technology and expertise, it can improve an organization's ability to support globalization, and it can reduce compliance risks. But the process itself must be well planned and well executed, or it can fail.

This book contains the most current and comprehensive information on HR outsourcing that is available today. Many of the ideas and techniques have been created and used to assist some of the largest companies in America and are being shared here for the first time. Following are a few highlights of what you will gain from reading this book. You will:

- Discover what your peers are doing.

- Learn how to establish an outsourcing plan.

- Find out how to identify functional candidates for outsourcing.

- Learn how to define your requirements.

- Read about structuring service-level agreements.

- Find assistance in identifying potential vendors.

- Acquire templates for drafting requests for information, and requests for proposals, and contracts.

- Gain insight into making an outsourcing decision.

- Benefit from experienced contracting advice.

- Expand your expertise in vendor management.

- Peer into the future of outsourcing and its effect on HR.

The CD-ROM accompanying this book contains additional materials to help you in your outsourcing project. There is a list of often-used acronyms, a complete glossary of HR and outsourcing terms, and sample materials and agreements that will prevent you from re-inventing the outsourcing wheel.

Anyone who is in business or who is currently working in a corporate or government environment will benefit from the expertise and knowledge provided in this book and the accompanying CD-ROM. It is state-of-the-art information from leading consultants in the field of outsourcing HR functions.

Acknowledgments

We wish to thank the people who supported the creation of this book. They are the best and brightest people to have around when you work on this type of project, and we jointly thank them for their efforts, their intelligence, and their good humor throughout the process.

This book would never have been completed without the diligent and painstaking efforts of Angela Chevalier, Julie Ivan, and Micha Jakub in the research and production of the tables, charts, and text of this manuscript. In addition, we drew heavily on the experience of other senior consultants and experts in this field who took the time to review and edit many of the chapters in this book. Thank you to our co-workers Debbie Card, Rosemary Collins, Jeff Croyle, Janet Grogan, Jeff Krynski, Mark Lawson, Dave Mortell, and David Stacy and to Peter Whalley of BP and Mike McClory of Bullard Smith for your thoughtful contributions.

Introduction

Today, all around the globe, HR executives are considering or are actively engaged in outsourcing all or part of the HR function. Significant advances in technology have created a situation where work and most jobs can be done anywhere in the world. This globalization of jobs has come about because thousands of companies trying to compete in a global economy have found highly educated work forces in places such as India and China, where salaries are much lower and benefits are more affordable. Thus, leaders in every industry are reshaping their organizations through outsourcing, offshoring, and nearshoring, and their strategy includes the HR function.

Outsourcing has also evolved from the original idea of being purely a cost-saving strategy into an effective strategic management tool that most organizations must use in order to remain competitive in the global marketplace. When outsourcing is thoughtfully introduced to an organization and masterfully executed, it optimizes all business processes; expands an organization's capabilities, both technical and otherwise; and builds a competitive advantage.

Outsourcing allows service providers to reduce costs-thanks to leverage-because they perform work for more than one company. Business process outsourcing providers can provide economies of scale by leveraging their technology, aggregating their purchasing power, and sharing their specialized resources. Therefore, they can provide lower migration costs for the buyer because the service provider doesn't have to keep reinventing the wheel.

Early outsourcing efforts now seem simple when one views the huge global outsourcing activities of large corporations today such as IBM, Bank of America, Best Buy, BP, Goodyear, Motorola, PepsiCo, Procter & Gamble, and Sun Microsystems-just to name a few. As outsourcing becomes the rule rather than the exception, more long-term strategic relationships are being forged, and more and more companies are moving a variety of formerly in-house processes to off shore so they can achieve higher performance at lower cost.

Federal and state governments are also enthusiastically outsourcing HR functions. The federal government now spends about $100 billion more annually on outside contracts than it does on employee salaries. Many federal departments and offices such as the National Aeronautics and Space Administration and the Energy Department, to name just two, have become de facto contract management agencies as they devote upward of 80 percent of their budgets to contractors.

Outsourcing is ultimately changing the way in which business is transacted, functions are managed, and management roles and responsibilities are assigned. It enables companies to shift from vertically integrated islands to complex matrixes of interrelationship. Selecting, contracting, and managing this web of providers and services is one of the most crucial challenges that companies face today. We hope this book will provide a comprehensive easy-to-use roadmap in your pursuit of organizational excellence through outsourcing.

OUTSOURCING HUMAN RESOURCES FUNCTIONS

PART I

Identifying Critical Outsourcing
Issues, Making the Decision,
and Establishing a Plan

CHAPTER 1
What Is HR Outsourcing?

Human resource (HR) outsourcing means having a third-party service provider or vendor administer, on an ongoing basis, an HR activity that would normally be performed internally. A vendor will contract to perform a specific HR activity, thus delivering predetermined services for an established fee. The following are three characteristics to consider before successfully outsourcing of an HR activity:

1. The work can be performed by an external third party, possibly at lower cost.

2. Credible service providers have the requisite skill, technology, and subject matter expertise to perform the work.

3. It is possible to negotiate a contractual agreement that will bind a provider to perform the services under a service level agreement at a predetermined cost.

Outsourcing, including HR outsourcing, is a technique that is frequently used by organizations to gain a competitive advantage. Although you do lose some control of daily activities, you will reduce costs, which is usually an outsourcing objective. There are many other reasons for your organization to consider outsourcing, including these:

- Improving the quality of the services provided by gaining access to a specialist

- Avoiding capital investments in technology that would be required to provide the services

- Having an inability to sustain the requisite staff members because your organization lacks career opportunities internally

- Gaining access to new value-added services, technology, or features that your organization cannot provide internally

- Increasing the scalability of the HR function so that your organization reacts more effectively to the changing needs of the business

- Restructuring an existing HR function that may no longer meet the needs of your organization

- Decreasing the conflicting demands on the internal information technology (IT) function so that it can focus on core business activities

- Improving your organization's ability to assimilate mergers and acquisitions

- Simplifying and codifying policies and procedures

- Converting the delivery function to one that has a transparent cost structure and that delivers its homogeneous service with quality and according to prescribed metrics

Why Outsource?

Given the complexity, cost, and highly regulated nature of the HR function, most companies have started to outsource HR activities for various reasons. Many companies find that using outside service providers to recruit and hire staff members, to process payroll, to administer benefit programs, to deliver training, or to support their HR systems environment is more efficient and less costly than hiring staff members to handle those complex functions internally. Companies are constantly looking for ways to cut functional overhead costs and increasingly are turning to outsourcing as a solution. Experts predict that the HR outsourcing market will grow at nearly a 10 percent compound annual rate over the next several years, thus resulting in more than a $100 billion market worldwide by 2010.

Another reason that many companies turn to outsourcing is to improve the quality of services provided to their employees. Unlike internal HR administration functions, outsourcing service providers must compete in the marketplace to earn the right to provide those services. One way that providers try to distinguish themselves is by providing new technology, better tools, or value-added services that are not commonly available. Outsourcing vendors are able to offer those enhanced services because they can leverage technology investments across all of their clients, which, in turn, allows them to make investments that no single organization could justify on its own.

More recently, a third reason has emerged that is driving yet another wave of outsourcing in HR: the desire by companies to restructure the HR function so that the remaining internal staff is much more focused on strategic activities (such as developing the executive talent in the organization) and is less mired in transactional administration. Although it is possible to transform HR either internally or externally, the external option of outsourcing often enables companies to achieve their objectives more quickly and at a lower cost.

Figures 1.1 and 1.2 provide a snapshot of many factors that cause companies to decide to outsource their HR activities.

Figure 1.1
Reasons for HR Outsourcing

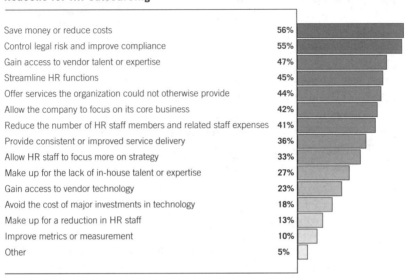

Save money or reduce costs	56%
Control legal risk and improve compliance	55%
Gain access to vendor talent or expertise	47%
Streamline HR functions	45%
Offer services the organization could not otherwise provide	44%
Allow the company to focus on its core business	42%
Reduce the number of HR staff members and related staff expenses	41%
Provide consistent or improved service delivery	36%
Allow HR staff to focus more on strategy	33%
Make up for the lack of in-house talent or expertise	27%
Gain access to vendor technology	23%
Avoid the cost of major investments in technology	18%
Make up for a reduction in HR staff	13%
Improve metrics or measurement	10%
Other	5%

Reprinted from *Human Resources Outsourcing Survey Report*, SHRM Survey Program, p. 4 (2004),
with permission from Society for Human Resource Management.

Figure 1.2
Anticipated Results of Outsourcing HR Activities

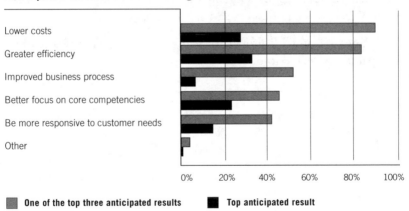

Lower costs
Greater efficiency
Improved business process
Better focus on core competencies
Be more responsive to customer needs
Other

0%   20%   40%   60%   80%   100%

■ **One of the top three anticipated results**   ■ **Top anticipated result**

Reprinted by permission of the publisher from *Strategic Sourcing Implications for Human Resources*
(Hewitt Associates LLC, 2004), 5.

Advantages and Disadvantages of HR Outsourcing

Outsourcing has both advantages and disadvantages. In many ways, the reasons for outsourcing (described earlier) can also be considered the advantages of outsourcing. But what are the disadvantages? Most companies fear either a loss of control or the potential for a degradation of service to their employees. In addition, some companies have experienced unexpected costs while outsourcing.

Figure 1.3 lists the most common obstacles faced by clients who have outsourced HR functions. Many of those obstacles can be considered potential disadvantages of outsourcing.

Figure 1.3
Obstacles Faced in Decision to Outsource HR Functions

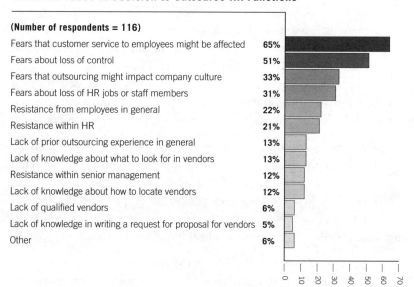

(Number of respondents = 116)	
Fears that customer service to employees might be affected	65%
Fears about loss of control	51%
Fears that outsourcing might impact company culture	33%
Fears about loss of HR jobs or staff members	31%
Resistance from employees in general	22%
Resistance within HR	21%
Lack of prior outsourcing experience in general	13%
Lack of knowledge about what to look for in vendors	13%
Resistance within senior management	12%
Lack of knowledge about how to locate vendors	12%
Lack of qualified vendors	6%
Lack of knowledge in writing a request for proposal for vendors	5%
Other	6%

Note: Percentages do not total 100 percent because respondents were allowed to indicate multiple response options. Results are based on responses from HR professionals who are from organizations that currently outsource one or more HR functions and who reported facing obstacles when deciding to outsource.

Reprinted from *Human Resources Outsourcing Survey Report*, SHRM Survey Program, p. 5 (2004), with permission from Society for Human Resource Management.

It is interesting to review the responses carefully. Upon inspection, it becomes apparent that most disadvantages of outsourcing could alternatively be attributed to difficulties in either establishing or managing the outsourcing relationship. Perhaps the disadvantages even reflect that some adopters of outsourcing fail to appreciate the need for their organization to make changes in conjunction with the necessary changes in their delivery strategy. In fact, you will not find any strategic disadvantages on the list. Therefore, the challenge for HR professionals would appear to be their need to learn how to establish and manage outsourcing relationships effectively.

Alternatives for Outsourcing

The term *outsourcing* is generally used today in its broadest sense and encompasses a multitude of different types of client–provider relationships. To add to the potential confusion, the various media increasingly treat *outsourcing* as being synonymous with *offshoring*, which is an entirely different concept (see Chapter 21). For this book, we will be more specific and consistent in our use of those words.

In particular, we will identify the following separate and distinct types of third-party sourcing that an organization might use and that are relevant in the HR marketplace today. The type of outsourcing arrangement that's appropriate for your organization will depend on a combination of your strategic objectives and of the nature of the vendor market that provides the services you plan to outsource.

Subprocess outsourcing. This term refers to outsourcing a single component of an HR process. An example of subprocess outsourcing might be the administration of the Consolidated Omnibus Budget Reconciliation Act (COBRA), in which a specialty provider handles the end-to-end COBRA process, but that process—in and of itself—is just a subprocess of administering health and welfare benefits.

Single-process outsourcing. This term refers to using a third-party provider for an entire HR process. The best example of single-process outsourcing would be in the benefits administration area, where it is possible to outsource virtually all aspects of administering defined benefit, defined contribution, or health and welfare plans.

Co-sourcing, or point solutions. This term refers to a sharing between a third party and an organization of the responsibilities for delivering one or more HR processes. Good examples of co-sourcing might include a third party's hosting a human resource information system (HRIS) platform or the use of a third-party provider for supporting employees in a call center. In both examples, responsibility for the process remains with the client organization, even though the third party is providing an important set of services related to that process. Note that application service provider (ASP) relationships are a form of co-sourcing.

Human resource outsourcing (HRO). This term refers to those solutions that have all of the following characteristics:

- The client is outsourcing at least workforce administration services (see Chapter 9).

- The client is converting its employee data to the third-party provider's HRIS platform, sometimes referred to as a *transform then transfer approach.*

- The client anticipates that the provider will continue to enhance its systems platform without the client's having a recurring capital investment. In fact, most HRO providers' long-term strategy is to develop a one-to-many systems platform that can support multiple clients simultaneously.

Business process outsourcing (BPO). This term refers to those solutions that have all of the following characteristics:

- The client is outsourcing at least workforce administration services.

- The third party is originally taking over the employee data from the client in the data's current form on the client's current HRIS platform, sometimes referred to as a *transfer then transform approach.*

- The third party anticipates primarily making incremental capital investments that will have an expected return on that investment within that specific client relationship.

Note that we have excluded a couple of types of third-party relationships from the definitions. In particular, we do not consider the purchase and installation of a software program to be a form of outsourcing because the client retains the responsibility for all services using that software.

The trend in today's marketplace is toward greater overall integration on many levels. Organizations are looking to migrate from subprocess outsourcing toward single-process outsourcing or even to comprehensive HRO and BPO relationships. Companies are seeking integrated systems and services and want to reduce the number of vendor relationships that they must coordinate and manage.

What HR Functions Should or Should Not Be Outsourced?

Many organizations struggle with the decision of what functions they should consider outsourcing. This decision-making process gets a little easier when they consider the purpose of outsourcing: to gain a competitive advantage. This same consideration can be used to distinguish what services should be retained internally. In other words, organizations should retain functions as long as they can demonstrate that an internal solution provides a competitive advantage over all external alternatives. Under this definition, the internal solution must be better, cheaper, and sustainable. Otherwise, the function is an appropriate candidate for outsourcing.

Another way to begin to identify functions that are candidates for outsourcing is to observe what peer organizations are doing. Table 1.1 illustrates the relative use of outsourcing by organizations today.

There are some commonly accepted reasons that companies should refrain from outsourcing certain HR functions. Figure 1.4 illustrates some of the more common reasons that companies decide not to outsource various HR functions.

As shown in the figure, there are two primary reasons that functions should not be outsourced:

1. The market is not yet sufficiently mature enough to justify outsourcing the function because the services can still be performed more effectively internally from a cost or quality perspective.

2. The function is perceived as strategically too important for the business to outsource.

Determining the maturity of the outsourcing market requires looking at the specific services under consideration in conjunction

Table 1.1
Use of Outsourcing by Process

RESPONSES (%)

Function	Outsource Completely	Outsource Partially	Do Not Outsource	Average Years Outsourced
Background or criminal background checks	49	24	27	5
Employee assistance or counseling	47	19	35	7
Flexible spending account administration	43	24	33	6
Consolidated Omnibus Budget Reconciliation Act administration	38	17	45	5
Health care benefits administration	24	36	40	8
Temporary staffing	21	33	46	7
Pension benefits administration	19	36	45	8
Retirement benefits administration	17	30	54	8
Employee relocation	13	16	71	6
Payroll administration	13	35	52	8
Retirement planning	11	10	80	9
Work-life balance benefits administration	6	5	89	4
Compensation or incentive plans administration	4	15	82	7
Executive development and coaching	4	16	80	6
Human resource information system development	4	11	85	5
Recruitment or staffing of nonexecutive employees	4	26	71	6
Recruitment or staffing of executives	4	24	73	7
Risk management	4	8	88	8
Expatriate administration	2	4	94	6
Employee communication of plans or strategies	1	9	90	5
Performance management	1	2	97	6
Training and development programs	1	20	80	6
Policy development or implementation	0	4	96	5
Strategic business planning	0	4	96	2

Note: Number of respondents = 168. Percentages are row percentages and may not total 100 percent because of rounding. Data are based on organizations that currently outsource one or more HR function. The percentages are not adjusted to reflect cases in which an organization may not perform a particular HR function. Average number of years outsourced includes outsourcing of HR functions both partially and completely.

Reprinted from *Human Resources Outsourcing Survey Report*, SHRM Survey Program, p. 3 (2004), with permission from Society for Human Resource Management.

Figure 1.4
Reasons for Not HR Outsourcing

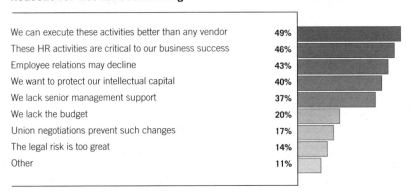

We can execute these activities better than any vendor	**49%**
These HR activities are critical to our business success	**46%**
Employee relations may decline	**43%**
We want to protect our intellectual capital	**40%**
We lack senior management support	**37%**
We lack the budget	**20%**
Union negotiations prevent such changes	**17%**
The legal risk is too great	**14%**
Other	**11%**

Reprinted by permission of the publisher from *Strategic Sourcing Implications for Human Resources* (Hewitt Associates LLC, 2004), 9.

with considering the size of the organization seeking to outsource those functions. Chapters 2 through 8 explain the process for reaching this determination.

Some HR activities that are generally accepted as being poor candidates for outsourcing include these:

- Employee relations

- Labor relations and negotiations

- Compensation and benefits plan design

- Employee communication strategy

- Diversity planning, training, and recruitment

- Executive talent development

- Organizational development planning

Although some organizations do outsource these functions, most find it necessary to keep them in house in order to maintain control of the corporate culture and HR strategy or because the organizations perceive that these functions require a level of discretion that makes them poor candidates for outsourcing.

The Outsourcing Life Cycle

Outsourcing is a dynamic solution for providing business services. The marketplace for services is always evolving, changing, and combining as vendors seek to develop more attractive services that they can offer their clients. Therefore, if you are to maximize the value of outsourcing for your organization, it is helpful to use a life cycle approach toward establishing and monitoring your vendor relationships. This life cycle includes the following steps:

- Creating a vision for outsourcing

- Assessing the feasibility of outsourcing

- Identifying and selecting the right service provider

- Contracting with the provider

- Governing, or managing, the provider relationship

- Benchmarking the provider's services

- Renewing or replacing the provider at the end of the contract

This book will more fully describe how to effectively execute and monitor an outsourcing strategy while using the life cycle approach.

CHAPTER 2
Making an Outsourcing Decision

Understanding the strategic implications and practical steps that you should take when deciding to outsource is important. You should weigh the advantages against the risks carefully and thoughtfully, because outsourcing decisions usually represent a permanent change in strategy and have long-term implications. Careful analysis is required to ensure that the outsourcing strategy will meet your organization's financial and business objectives and to confirm that the vendor marketplace can sustain or exceed current service levels. In addition, it is important to focus on the process of outsourcing and the timing of the change. Such a significant change in the way that a company does business should come in stages that can be planned, implemented, and managed successfully over time.

Understanding the Nature of the Decision

The first step in making the decision to outsource is to clearly identify the nature of the decision. In particular, are you making a basic, tactical "make versus buy" decision, or are you potentially pointing your organization in a new strategic direction from which you are unlikely to return. For example, the decision to hire an external recruiter to outsource some of your staffing requirements can be easily reversed, and such a decision can stand on its own merits. Conversely, outsourcing a more complex area such as defined benefit administration—particularly if it involves a conversion to a vendor's proprietary systems platform—is a strategic decision that is likely to be maintained into perpetuity. So although the decision-making process follows the same steps, strategic outsourcing decisions deserve more care, due diligence, and management concurrence than do tactical outsourcing decisions.

Visioning

Strategic outsourcing decisions—those decisions that change the delivery strategy of an organization—typically go through a preliminary analysis phase. This phase of considering outsourcing is often called a *visioning phase*. Usually a feasibility study is done at this point. The objectives of this phase are as follows:

- Identify the specific services that can be outsourced in support of the strategic objectives that have been established.

- Identify the systems and technological functionality that might be acquired through outsourcing.

- Identify the kind of cost savings or productivity improvements that would be required to support the decision to outsource the function.

- Begin to consider the effect that outsourcing would have on the organization and the change management that would need to be performed.

Although it is relatively easy to identify those noncore functions that can and perhaps should be outsourced in an academic sense, many organizations need to come to this conclusion as part of an overall educational process. The most common approach used to identify the processes that should be outsourced is a visioning exercise. Visioning entails holding a series of discussions to identify the potential for outsourcing within any given HR function. The process starts with identifying strategic versus transactional activities within the function. Ideally, all transactional activities would be included in the analysis of the outsourcing alternative. The decision to retain specific activities that are potentially strategic for the organization can be made after the vendors' capabilities have been taken into account, later in the process. Visioning provides a useful framework for a broad segment of the HR functional leaders to openly discuss and analyze their processes in a creative environment. This visioning exercise can be a valuable first step in the outsourcing process.

Defining the Scope of Services for Consideration

The most important step in any outsourcing decision-making process is to clearly define the scope of the services that are being considered for outsourcing. Too often, organizations make the mistake of assuming that there is an industry standard definition of outsourcing for various services. However, the outsourcing marketplace for most HR services has developed to satisfy a wide variety of potential clients. Thus, the potential providers for any specific service will include software application developers; outsourcing providers for the small, middle, or large markets; co-sourcing organizations; third-party administrators; and consulting firms. To the extent that those organizations successfully address the needs of their specific target market, they will believe that they are in the general outsourcing marketplace for the services you require.

For example, it is not uncommon for companies to issue a request for proposal (RFP) for payroll services only to find that it is very difficult to compare services and prices, given the variation in the marketplace for defining in-scope versus out-of-scope services. But for small companies, payroll administration merely involves producing payroll checks and advices on a schedule, including determining and reporting tax and other deductions. However, larger companies may want their payroll administrator to perform customer service functions related to changes in tax elections, to administer garnishments, or even to provide data files to other organizations. So it is easy to see how misunderstandings can arise between purchasers and sellers of outsourced services.

To avoid this confusion—or, worse yet, the establishment of a relationship that does not meet the needs of your organization—you must take the time to develop a detailed set of requirements for the function you are interested in outsourcing. Chapter 4 describes a simple and effective process for capturing and communicating your business requirements.

Calculating Baseline Costs

The next step, after identifying your business requirements, is to calculate the baseline cost of administration prior to outsourcing. Although the ultimate decision to outsource may depend largely on nonfinancial factors, such as a desire to gain access to modern technology, all outsourcing decisions require an analysis of the effect of the decision on operating costs.

Capturing the current (i.e., baseline) cost of administration in such a way that it can be compared to the cost of outsourcing may prove more complex than originally envisioned. Every organization tracks its internal costs in a way that makes the most sense for that particular organization. Outsourcing organizations, however, tend to track their costs on a client-by-client basis so that they can assess the profitability of each assignment. Therefore, their model will be designed to specifically identify all of the costs related to the provision of administrative services.

Your organization may not be a service organization. It may be a large manufacturing or retail organization that is more interested in tracking the cost of inventory or goods produced. Thus, the internal budgets for staff functions like human resources may not contain all of the costs associated with performing these services. Common examples of relevant cost items that may not be included in HR functional budgets include rent, management overhead, IT support costs, HR systems operating costs, HR staff contained in business operating budgets, depreciation on capital investments, and third-party agreement fees and expenses. But all of those relevant costs must be captured in order to compare the cost of outsourcing to the current cost of administration internally.

There is a trick to ensuring that you have captured all of your current internal administrative costs. You should set up an analysis of your current costs as if you were an outsourcing provider. Under this approach, you would build your analysis to include the following broad categories of costs:

Direct staff expenses. This category includes all of the costs associated with the functional staff that is directly involved in providing the services.

Table 2.1

Inventory of Delivery Costs by Category

CATEGORY	DESCRIPTION
Direct staff expenses:	
Salary	Cost of base pay, overtime, shift differential, or any similar basic pay
Other compensation	Cost of annual bonus, stock bonus commissions, or any similar incentive pay
Pension, savings, and other	Allocated cost of defined benefit, profit-sharing, defined contribution, retirement benefits 401k, and retiree medical and life insurance benefits
Life, medical, and other benefits	Allocated cost of medical, dental, disability, life insurance, and other benefits
Wage-related taxes	Cost of FICA, federal and state unemployment, and any other employer-paid taxes
Rent and utilities	Allocated cost of basic rent, utilities, and operating charges
Travel and hotel expenses	Budgeted cost of airfare, meal, hotel, and other travel expenses
Office equipment	If expensed annually, the budgeted cost of any furniture, fixtures, or equipment; if amortized, the budgeted depreciation of prior purchases
Other office and occupancy expenses	Budgeted cost of nonstaff items such as business insurance, office supplies, repairs, maintenance of equipment, business taxes, permits, telephones, and postage
Other staff expenses	Budgeted cost of search fees, moving expenses, service awards, gifts, seminars, newspaper announcements or advertisements, publications, professional dues, and so forth
Operating expenses:	
Computer operations	Allocated cost of processing time, disk space, tape loads and storage, file transfers, online access, off-site backups, disaster recovery plans, and so forth
Software licenses	Cost of software leases, royalties, licenses, and maintenance agreements
Financial services	Cost of banking fees, lockboxes, tax reporting services, and so forth
Printing and mailing	Cost of printing, fulfillment, and cost of materials (such as paper stock), plus the cost of any handwork or subcontracted printing and fulfillment
Records retention	Cost of any off-site records storage or the rent associated with internal storage if not included above
Postage and shipping	Estimated cost of postage and shipping
Tolls and DSL)	Cost of 800 number usage, plus any dedicated lines (e.g., T-1 or telecommunications or other telecommunications charges (e.g., voice response usage fees)
External service providers:	
Professional services	Cost of actuarial, legal, accounting, or similar fees that are attributable to administrative activities
Temporary labor	Cost of temporary services and independent contractors
Third-party suppliers	Cost for any subcontracted or outsourced services (significant suppliers should be broken out individually)
Indirect internal staff and expenses:	
Overhead	Allocated cost of any divisional, company, or corporate overhead charges
Information systems	Estimated cost for services provided by internal systems support resources not included in the direct staff expenses above (e.g., desktop support, systems or data analysts, computer operators, and systemsdevelopers)
Field staff	Estimated cost for services provided by other internal resources not included in the direct staff expenses above (e.g., HR generalists in field locations contained in those unit operating budgets, rather than in the HR budget)
Other internal functions	Estimated cost for services provided by other internal resources not budgeted in direct staff costs above (e.g., internal audit, procurement, benefits accounting, legal, communications, or training)

Operating expenses. This category includes all of the nonstaff expenses associated with providing the services.

External service providers. This category includes all of the third-party costs (if any) already associated with providing the services.

Indirect staff expenses. This category consists of additional staff costs that are contained in other functional budgets within your organization, such as the IT and legal budget or the budgets of various field locations.

It is important to capture all of the costs necessary to provide the services being considered for outsourcing. Table 2.1 provides a more detailed description of each of the elements of cost that may be included in these major categories.

Once baseline costs are developed, the next step is to compare them against market benchmark data. The purpose of this comparison is to get an idea—before you approach the provider community—of whether you are likely to be able to establish a positive business case for outsourcing. In addition, comparing your baseline costs against marketplace benchmarks can provide you with confirmation that you have, in fact, identified all of your costs. Otherwise, your numbers may look unusual relative to the benchmark data.

There are several ways to develop benchmark data for comparison purposes. First, you may want to contact peer organizations to see if they have analyzed their functional costs. Second, you may want to review published data through an Internet search. Third, you may want to approach associations or organizations that benchmark HR functions as one of their services. Or, finally, you can ask vendors to provide detailed cost information that is based on their experience with similar organizations seeking similar services.

Note that benchmark data, though a useful tool, require some careful validation before those data can be applied to your outsourcing decision-making process. In particular, most benchmark data include information taken from a wide variety of organizations without any attempt to segregate the data for comparability. Therefore, it is sometimes necessary to adjust the benchmark data, either explicitly or implicitly, before using them in a direct comparison against your baseline costs.

Three factors that have a significant effect on benchmark data are

1. Size of the organization

2. Complexity of the services provided

3. Volume of activity of the services under consideration

Of those three, the first and last have the greatest effect on most HR activities. For example, the cost of administration for a firm with 100,000 employees, on a per employee basis, is likely to be 50 to 75 percent of the same cost for a firm with just 10,000 employees, and possibly less than half of the cost of a firm with 1,000 employees.

Program complexity also affects the cost of HR administration, although less than is commonly assumed. Generally, complexity will increase the cost of administration by 5 to 15 percent relative to industry standard pricing for any consistent set of services and size of organization.

Finally, not all organizations must support the same volume of activity in various HR functions. For example, a retailer that has 100 percent annual turnover has different requirements for its recruiting and staffing function than does a high-technology organization that has 10 percent turnover and is primarily concerned about hiring the best software engineers.

For all of those reasons, it can be difficult to find benchmarking data that are specific enough for comparison against cost baselines. Increasingly, however, such information is becoming available as more organizations monetize the cost of their administration by outsourcing.

Identifying Strategic Alternatives

The next step in analyzing the feasibility of outsourcing is to identify the various strategic alternatives. At a minimum, you should analyze the following alternatives:

The status quo scenario. Keep delivery in its current state, with minimal investment in new or enhanced capabilities.

The sustainable scenario. As in the case of the status quo scenario, keep delivery in its current state, but allow for a reasonable amount of investment in new technology to provide market-competitive services to employees.

A co-sourcing scenario. For example, implement a new point solution, such as sourcing certain aspects of the services like call center support to an external organization.

The outsourcing scenario. Shift responsibility for the day-to-day management of the function under consideration to a third-party organization.

Note that the objective of modeling those alternatives is not really to compare and contrast them as equivalent options for consideration but (a) to identify whether outsourcing the function is feasible and (b) to provide a reasonable amount of due diligence on the outsourcing alternative by reviewing other options available to the organization. Some may disagree with establishing this objective, but having such a specific purpose is critical to driving the analysis to a recommendation and a decision. In the long run, effective outsourcing markets will provide higher levels of service at a cheaper cost than an internal solution. If studying the feasibility of outsourcing cannot demonstrate this fact, then the market for the services is not sufficiently mature, and the results of the study clearly indicate that an organization may want to wait for those dynamics to change.

Note that historically there are few examples of outsourcing HR administration that have not ultimately yielded lower costs and higher-quality delivery. Thus, the answer to whether you should outsource depends merely on where the particular market you are analyzing is on the evolutionary curve. This philosophy leads to the point of emphasis already discussed. The purpose of a feasibility study is to determine whether outsourcing is an effective strategy for your organization to adopt today. If not, then your organization can use the feasibility study results to decide how long it may be before outsourcing becomes a feasible option for your firm. Studying the feasibility of outsourcing, therefore, provides useful input into future decisions with respect to additional capital investments in new HR technology.

Pay special attention to the elimination of theoretical solutions, because the status quo scenario is often not sustainable. In other words, the current systems applications may no longer be supportable or may be supportable only with significant levels of new capital investments. If so, the sustainable scenario should really be used as the status quo against which the outsourcing scenario is compared. Otherwise, it is possible that your organization will reach an erroneous conclusion that is based on a flawed analysis of the information.

Modeling the Alternatives

The next step is to model the financial business case for each of the four alternatives. To analyze the business case, you should do the following:

- Identify the time period for the analysis.

- Select the discount rate to use for the analysis.

- Estimate the internal and external transition costs associated with each alternative.

- Estimate the capital expenditures that will be required to sustain each alternative.

- Estimate the internal baseline costs that will be eliminated under each alternative.

Because outsourcing decisions often represent strategic changes in direction, it is reasonable to use a relatively long time horizon for the analysis. Time horizons of seven to ten years are not unreasonable for large-scale outsourcing decisions. However, time horizons of five to seven years are more common.

Business cases for outsourcing usually require the analysis of different patterns of cost. For example, an organization may incur increased costs in the short run during the transition to the external provider and then may enjoy reduced costs of operation once the transition is completed. The most common way to adjust for these timing differences is to use a net present value approach. Your organization's finance department is almost certain to have a specific rate that it will want you to use when calculating the net present value. If no rate guidance is available, 7 percent is commonly used as a discount rate in such analyses.

Estimating the internal and external transition costs can be difficult and may require interaction with other internal departments or external sources. Transition costs are the one-time costs associated with moving from the current environment to the new alternative environment. Examples of transition costs include

- Consulting fees for supporting the vendor selection process

- Legal fees for negotiating an agreement with the provider

- Vendor implementation fees

- Incremental internal travel or staff costs required to support the implementation

- Internal severance or retention costs

The next step is usually performed as a joint activity with the IT department. It involves projecting the amount and timing of the investments that your company will have to make to enhance or replace IT systems during the period of analysis. You may want to develop two different projections of those costs: the first that represents the minimum level of investment required to sustain the current environment and a second that reflects the level of investment necessary to maintain a market-competitive level of HR services.

Next, you must determine the adjustments to the baseline cost that would result from the change to the new delivery model. Ideally, you would reduce the baseline cost explicitly to reflect reductions in staff and the elimination of operating expenses, and you would add in the expected level of vendor fees. However, you could take a simpler approach and merely adjust the baseline cost to reflect the level of savings that your benchmarking analysis suggests can be achieved by outsourcing.

The final step is to assemble all of the components into a pro forma business case for each alternative. The changes in the cost components should be summed, and the net change in cost from each status quo scenario should be identified. Those changes should then be discounted to develop the net present value for each scenario. The scenario with the lowest net present value will be the preferred strategy, unless other nonfinancial considerations must be taken into account. Nonfinancial considerations are described in the next section.

Considering Nonfinancial Justifications for Outsourcing

Ideally, the outsourcing business case will yield the greatest cost savings over the time period under consideration. However, sometimes another scenario might lead to lower costs, particularly when the outsourcing market for the particular services under consideration is at an early stage of evolution. In those instances, it may still make sense to outsource if there are other beneficial consequences. Following is a list of possible overall business reasons to outsource even if the specific business case for HR is not compelling:

Ability to free up IT capacity for more important projects. Although it may be cheaper if your own IT personnel built or maintained the HR systems required to provide the services, they may have to do so at the expense of other projects that are more intrinsic to the business, such as improving the inventory system. Therefore, the opportunity cost associated with having your own IT staff work on HR systems ought to be considered.

Increased productivity, satisfaction among employees, or both. To the extent a vendor can provide better accessibility through self-service or a call center infrastructure, outsourcing may enable employees to perform certain HR functions at home or on weekends. Implicitly, this advantage can improve employees' productivity during normal business hours.

Elimination of leakage within financial programs. With respect to the transfer of information, vendor systems often operate with fewer time lags. Eliminating the time lags related to reporting changes in the status of employees allows more accurate reporting of health care plan eligibility, reporting of paid time-off allocations, collection of premium billings, and so forth. In turn, more accurate reporting can save real program dollars. In some cases, the savings you can achieve by tightening the links between the systems will far outweigh the incremental cost of providing the services.

Elimination or reduction of compliance risk. Certain HR functions contain a disproportionate amount of risk related to noncompliance with government rules and regulations. A simple example would be the financial risks associated with noncompliance with COBRA. Outsourcing vendors are expected to make ensuring compliance with government requirements part of their normal business operations.

Building Your Presentation to Management

The final step is to assimilate the results of your analysis into a presentation to management. Your presentation to management should cover the following topics:

- A description of the services being considered for outsourcing

- A summary of the results of the benchmarking analysis for costs and quality relative to marketplace norms and best practices

- A description of each of the strategic alternatives you analyzed

- A summary of the results of the business case analysis

- An assessment of the risks and the available options for mitigating those risks

- A timeline for the change

- A description of the pattern of capital and internal resource requirements

- A discussion of the change management implications for the organization

- Your recommendation, which is based on your conclusions

The objective of this presentation should be to secure management's support of either a recommendation to proceed with the next phase of the outsourcing process or to reach an explicit decision to pursue one of the other alternatives. Feasibility studies tend to generate momentum toward a decision, and that momentum may be wasted if you make a purely informational presentation with the hope of revisiting the subject for a decision at another time.

Managing Expectations

It is never too soon to start managing expectations associated with an outsourcing initiative. A common mistake is to view outsourcing as a simple "make versus buy" type of decision. Outsourcing usually represents a significant change in the way services are performed, often involving the following:

- A realignment of relationships among the HR staff, employees, and management,

- An introduction of new processes, procedures, and systems

- The establishment of new performance expectations for HR employees

- The creation of new roles and responsibilities related to vendor management within the HR organization

Such changes require leadership and management support to be successful. Change always brings with it a certain amount of disruption. The earlier the management team can be educated about the likely implications of outsourcing, the sooner the HR leadership team can begin planning to mitigate those concerns.

CHAPTER 3

Establishing an Outsourcing Plan

In the last chapter, we discussed the process that should be followed to assess the feasibility of outsourcing an HR function. In this chapter, we will assume that the feasibility study identified outsourcing as an effective alternative. This chapter describes in detail the next set of steps an organization should follow to identify and explore specific outsourcing options.

Setting Organizational Goals and Reaching Consensus

The first step at this stage of the outsourcing process is to define your organizational goals for the project. It is important to spend time on this activity before you start the vendor identification and selection process because those goals will influence many of the steps that follow. In particular, now is the time to begin to discuss internally the relative importance of several of the more significant drivers of outsourcing:

- How important is securing short- or long-term cost savings?

- How much interest does your organization have in gaining access to enhanced technology and capability?

- How much desire is there to refocus the internal staff from administrative to strategic activities?

- Can your organization avoid future capital investments in human resources that are otherwise required to sustain high-quality HR services?

- Can your organization secure a more scalable environment as it grows or shrinks?

Note that some of those items are in opposition. For example, gaining access to new technology or avoiding future capital investments may dilute outsourcing's potential for reducing short- or long-term delivery costs. Therefore, it is helpful to discuss the outsourcing drivers with management to get a relative sense of their importance before approaching the marketplace. Although it is not uncommon for priorities to change during an outsourcing assessment process, having a preliminary sense of their relative importance at the commencement of such a process is always helpful. Reaching agreement on these relative priorities will help to build consensus about the manner in which your organization approaches the vendor community and the decisions reached throughout the process.

Establishing a Timeline

The next step is to establish a timeline for the vendor evaluation and selection process. Refer to the Table 3.1 to construct the optimal amount of time needed for the vendor selection process. In Figure 3.1, we have provided estimates for the time requirements for both a simple HR function such as COBRA administration and a more complex function such as payroll administration. Larger projects, such as outsourcing all your HR delivery in a business process outsourcing strategy, will require additional time.

Table 3.1
Sample Vendor Selection Timeline

Step	Simple HR Function	Complex HR Function
Define requirements	2 weeks	4 weeks
Draft request for proposal	3 weeks	4 weeks
Allow time for vendors to respond	2-3 weeks	3-4 weeks
Evaluate proposals	1-2 weeks	2-3 weeks
Conduct site visits and due diligence	3-4 weeks	4-6 weeks
Make recommendations to management	1 week	2 weeks
Total length of process	**12-15 weeks**	**19-23 weeks**

Figure 3.1
Vendor Selection Process Flow

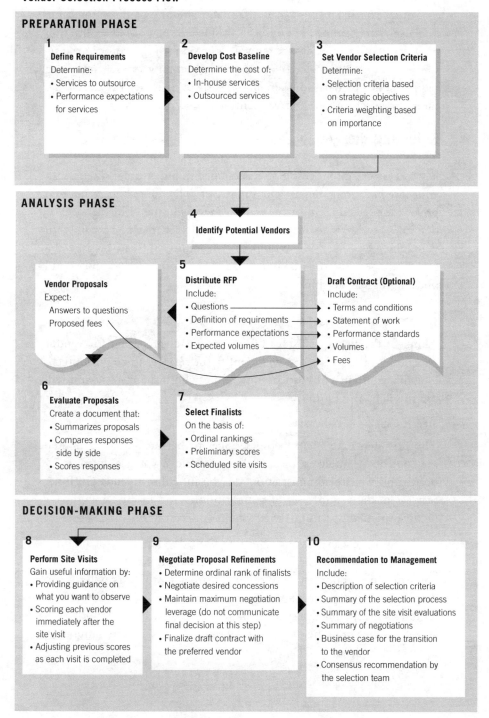

PREPARATION PHASE

1
Define Requirements
Determine:
• Services to outsource
• Performance expectations
  for services

2
Develop Cost Baseline
Determine the cost of:
• In-house services
• Outsourced services

3
Set Vendor Selection Criteria
Determine:
• Selection criteria based
  on strategic objectives
• Criteria weighting based
  on importance

ANALYSIS PHASE

4
Identify Potential Vendors

5
Vendor Proposals
Expect:
  Answers to questions
  Proposed fees

Distribute RFP
Include:
• Questions
• Definition of requirements
• Performance expectations
• Expected volumes

Draft Contract (Optional)
Include:
• Terms and conditions
• Statement of work
• Performance standards
• Volumes
• Fees

6
Evaluate Proposals
Create a document that:
• Summarizes proposals
• Compares responses
  side by side
• Scores responses

7
Select Finalists
On the basis of:
• Ordinal rankings
• Preliminary scores
• Scheduled site visits

DECISION-MAKING PHASE

8
Perform Site Visits
Gain useful information by:
• Providing guidance on
  what you want to observe
• Scoring each vendor
  immediately after the
  site visit
• Adjusting previous scores
  as each visit is completed

9
Negotiate Proposal Refinements
• Determine ordinal rank of finalists
• Negotiate desired concessions
• Maintain maximum negotiation
  leverage (do not communicate
  final decision at this step)
• Finalize draft contract with
  the preferred vendor

10
Recommendation to Management
Include:
• Description of selection criteria
• Summary of the selection process
• Summary of the site visit evaluations
• Summary of negotiations
• Business case for the transition
  to the vendor
• Consensus recommendation by
  the selection team

Some external factors may affect the amount of transition time available. For example, if you are considering payroll administration providers, you may want to time your decision so that you can transition to the new provider on January 1 to simplify the tax reporting requirements. Under those circumstances, you may need to accelerate the optimal schedules we have identified.

Selecting the Vendor

There are many approaches to selecting an outsourcing provider. The key to a successful process is to reach a decision that is consistent with your organization's needs and objectives. The following structured process for selecting an outsourcing vendor, illustrated in Figure 3-1, describes ten steps to making a clear choice that is consistent with your objectives. Working within this structure, you can manage the selection process to maximize your potential for a successful outsourcing partnership.

THE PREPARATION PHASE

Think of the first three steps in the process as preparing for vendor selection. In this phase, you will identify the services to be outsourced, establish your current cost baseline, and establish the criteria you will use to select a vendor.

Step 1: Defining Requirements

The first step is to identify the services to be outsourced. This step may not be as simple as it seems. For example, if you are outsourcing health and welfare administration, do you intend to include COBRA services in the vendor's set of responsibilities? Or inactive billing? Or flexible spending account (FSA) claims administration?

The way to clarify your objective is to develop a set of requirements. Those requirements are the expectations for the roles your company, the vendor, and any other third-party providers will play in delivering each aspect of the services you want to outsource. The requirements should also specify the performance expectation for each aspect of the work. The process of defining your business requirements is covered in detail in Chapter 4.

Step 2: Developing a Cost Baseline

The next step is to develop baseline cost information. If the function is already outsourced, it is fairly simple to determine the current cost of the services: simply analyze the contract fees plus any change orders that reflect recurring, ongoing work as opposed to implementation fees for changes to the services. If, however, this is the first time you will outsource the function, developing baseline costs is more complicated, as was described in Chapter 2.

Step 3: Setting Vendor Selection Criteria

Now establish vendor selection criteria for important items such as customer service, business relationship, access to advanced technology, or cost. Keep the number of selection criteria reasonably small— ideally fewer than ten. Each of the criteria should be weighted to reflect the relative importance of your objectives for the outsourcing project. This step is important because it is the point at which strategic objectives are incorporated into the decision-making process.

After completing these three steps (define requirements, develop cost baseline, set selection criteria), you should have crystallized an understanding of your company's objectives and a foundation on which the remainder of the process can rest.

THE ANALYSIS PHASE

Steps 4 through 7 constitute the analysis phase. In this phase, you will compare your requirements against each vendor's ability to satisfy them. The objective is to identify the vendor or vendors that can meet your needs and then to single out the one vendor that best satisfies your strategic objectives.

Step 4: Identifying Potential Vendors

The next step is to identify the vendors to be considered. This process is described in detail in Chapter 5. Depending on your selection criteria, you may need to contact only a few vendors. However, it is important not to let your preexisting biases affect which vendors are included. The outsourcing business is evolving rapidly, and vendors' service offerings have been known to change significantly over fairly short periods of time.

At the same time, there is no benefit in including a vendor that clearly cannot win the business. It is an expensive and time-consuming endeavor to respond to a request for proposal. No vendor, even one with an existing relationship with the client, wants to make that investment when the vendor has been included merely as a courtesy but without a realistic chance to be selected.

Step 5: Distributing the Request for Proposal

In step 5, you develop the RFP. When drafting an RFP, you must keep in mind the desired result: to establish a long-term business relationship that will be codified in a contract. The most common mistake is to separate the selection process from the contracting process. Any schism between those two processes introduces the possibility of a misunderstanding between the client and the vendor, potentially damaging the emerging strategic relationship between the two organizations. Chapter 6 provides a detailed roadmap for drafting an effective RFP.

Step 6: Evaluating Vendors' Proposal Responses

Once you receive the vendors' proposals, you will need to perform a detailed analysis of their fee and service responses. Ideally, you will have created an analysis framework while the vendors were developing their responses. Chapter 7 provides some guidance with respect to effective ways of comparing and contrasting proposals, particularly fee proposals. You may need to spend some time talking to the vendors during the evaluation process to clarify their written responses.

Step 7: Selecting Finalists

With the proposal summary and scoring complete, you will be prepared to give each vendor both an ordinal ranking and a preliminary score. Often, there is an obvious breakpoint, where two or three vendors' proposals clearly are superior. Those standout vendors usually are selected as finalists. However, it may be appropriate to substitute your incumbent or a vendor with whom you have an existing relationship in the place of one of the finalists. Although this approach is not strictly fair, it is a practical way either to dealing with the political reality within your organization or to reflect your confidence in a provider, given your prior experiences with that organization.

This stage may also be an appropriate time to revisit your original selection criteria. For example, many clients tend to place a lesser emphasis on cost in the early stages of a selection process. But once vendors have established their credibility for being able to satisfy the desired requirements, cost may play a larger role in decision making.

THE DECISION-MAKING PHASE

In the final phase of the process, you will reach a decision. Through the RFP responses of the vendors, you will have learned about their organizations and capabilities. But RFP responses generally do not provide a feel for how effectively the vendors perform their services— nor do they convey personal chemistry between members of the vendor's team and the client organization. Yet those factors are crucial for the long-term success of an outsourcing relationship. Therefore, it is wise to consider, first, the RFP as the tool for identifying finalists and, second, due diligence as the source of information to identify the preferred supplier.

Step 8: Performing Due Diligence

The next step is to perform a reasonable amount of due diligence to confirm or amplify your understanding of each finalist's proposal. The method used by most organizations to perform due diligence is to participate in a series of site visits to each finalist. Other interchanges with vendors can supplement the site visits as necessary. The due diligence phase of the process is an excellent opportunity to address issues and concerns that are unique to your organization but are outside the specific areas of expertise of the vendor selection team. For example, your IT department may be interested in the vendor's disaster recovery plan, or the legal department may be concerned about how the vendor manages data privacy.

Step 9: Negotiating Refinements to Proposals

The negotiation step is the critical juncture in the selection process. At this stage, there is maximum leverage to negotiate a favorable arrangement with the preferred vendor. On the one hand, the vendors have invested themselves in the proposal process and probably are emotionally committed to winning the business. On the other hand, as soon as you identify the recommended vendor, the leverage shifts from you to the vendor. Therefore, before you communicate the final selection decision, it is essential to tie up all loose ends. Those loose ends may include negotiating final fees, agreeing to key contract terms and conditions, modifying how the services will be performed and who will perform them, establishing performance reporting and standards, or addressing any other proposal refinement that you would like to secure.

Step 10: Developing Recommendation to Management

Finally, it is time to confirm the selection decision in a recommendation to management while seeking management's approval to negotiate an agreement with the provider. Using the cost baseline established in step 2, develop a business case to accompany the recommendation. A business case should reflect the following:

- The current cost of services

- A budget for the transition of services

- The cost of services after outsourcing

- A projection of those costs over a reasonable timeframe

In preparing the management recommendation, include these items:

- A description of the original selection criteria

- A summary of the process used to select finalists

- A summary of the evaluation of site visits

- A summary of the negotiations after the site visit

- The business case for the transition to the vendor

- A consensus recommendation by the selection team

- An assessment of the risks related to the recommendation

- A plan for the mitigation of those risks

Negotiating a Good Contract

Once you have secured management's approval, the next step is to negotiate the outsourcing agreement with the vendor. It is a good practice to complete the contract negotiations process as quickly as possible following the selection process. Ideally, the contract would be signed before the transition of services to the provider has commenced.

With luck, you will have already reached an agreement with your provider on most of the key contract terms and business issues as part of the vendor selection process. But the contracting process by its nature will tend to force any lingering issues to the surface to be resolved. The contracting team should expect some misunderstandings to arise and should be prepared to deal with them calmly but firmly. As long as the implementation has not commenced, your organization should still have sufficient negotiating leverage to ensure a fair resolution of any issues. The contracting process is described in detail in Chapter 17.

Communicating the Decision

Communication is a critical element for the success of any outsourcing project. If you started the process of communicating the potential ramifications of outsourcing during the feasibility study phase of the process, your task will be easier now. You will need the support of your management, your staff, and the rest of HR to complete the transition and to manage the change within the organization.

Identify points of time at which you'll communicate with both the HR staff and the entire company. Give some consideration to the methods of communication that you will use. One-on-one, written, email, or perhaps employee meetings are needed when you are ready to launch the outsourcing project. Most vendors will have experience with similar change management processes and may be able to provide resources or materials to assist with the communications.

Building a Rollout Schedule

The desired implementation schedule either will have been specified in the RFP or will have been recommended by the successful vendor. However, it is not uncommon for delays to occur in the decision-making process, thus requiring you to revisit the original project schedule.

Once the basic schedule is reset to account for any time lags, then you can refine the schedule to accommodate other business needs. For example, it may be beneficial to delay the implementation to coincide with the end of a calendar or fiscal year or to avoid a busy season such as budget preparation or holidays.

Revising the project schedule is essential to ensuring the perceived success of the outsourcing project. It is unrealistic to believe that the time will be made up during the implementation, because outsourcing implementations will tend to be complex. It is far easier to reset the schedule at the beginning of the outsourcing process while there is still a level of internal excitement about the decision than at the end of the implementation process after resources have been stretched, systems have been slated for elimination, and employee severance and retention agreements require modification.

Managing the Ongoing Relationship

As soon as the outsourcing decision has been reached, it is time to begin planning for the vendor management function. Ideally, the vendor relationship manager would be identified early in the process and would participate in the contract negotiations and the implementation. If an entire vendor management team is required, those employees will need to be identified during the implementation process to ensure that they remain with the company following the completion of the transition process. Chapter 18 provides detailed guidance with respect to the establishment of roles and responsibilities and the effective techniques for governance of an outsourcing relationship.

PART II

Defining Your Requirements, Selecting a Provider, and Communicating the Decision

CHAPTER 4

Defining Your Requirements

This chapter covers the most important step in the outsourcing process. An outsourcing relationship, by definition, is a business relationship between two parties. The more complex the services being provided are, the more important it becomes that both parties have an aligned interest in the success of the relationship and work together to maintain that alignment. This symbiotic relationship in outsourcing is sometimes called a *strategic partnership*.

Although one of the key ingredients for success in outsourcing is the establishment of a strategic partnership, that objective should never be substituted for the need to have a detailed definition of the requirements the provider is expected to fulfill. There are many examples of strategic partnerships that have gone awry because of a misunderstanding between the two organizations with respect to expectations.

The Service Delivery Model

The cornerstone of any outsourcing relationship is the *service delivery model*. In outsourcing vernacular, a service delivery model is the set of business requirements and performance expectations that the outsourcing vendor must satisfy. It is sometimes also called a *statement of work* and is often attached to the contractual agreement between the parties.

The purpose of a service delivery model is to explicitly describe the following:

- The services to be provided by the vendor

- The relative roles and responsibilities of the client, the vendor, and any third-party organizations in the provision of the services

- The performance expectations for every aspect of the services

If you use this format, you will be able to document the client–vendor relationship in a specific and concise format that captures the original intent of the two parties and that can also become the living definition of the relationship throughout the term of the agreement as amendments to the services are documented through a change control process (see Chapter 18).

DRAFTING A SERVICE DELIVERY MODEL

An outsourcing relationship can be difficult to describe, because it constitutes a set of services, rather than a product. For example, it would be easy to purchase a sports car by specifying that the car needed to seat two people and to be able to accelerate from 0 to 60 miles per hour in seven seconds or less. The first part of our description would be the requirement (i.e., a car that can seat two people), and the second part would be a performance expectation (i.e., that the car can accelerate from 0 to 60 miles per hour in seven seconds). We use the same approach to define the set of services that are required in an outsourcing relationship.

IDENTIFYING THE SERVICE DIMENSIONS

First, it is necessary to identify the various dimensions of an outsourcing relationship that need to be documented. Table 4.1 provides a sample description of the high-level dimensions of most outsourcing relationships. Each dimension shown in the table will be included as a section in the document. The last section, ad hoc services, shown in the table deserves some additional explanation. The primary objective of the service delivery model is to define the set of services that are "in scope" for the relationship—that is, the services that will be provided for the fees quoted by the vendor. However, in most outsourcing relationships, it is anticipated that additional services may be required under certain circumstances, such as when a new company is acquired. The ad hoc services section is used to document the vendor's obligation to support those additional out-of-scope services, even though the fee for those services will need to be determined at a future date as part of a change order.

Table 4.1
Dimensions of Outsourcing Relationships

SECTION	DESCRIPTION
Services and Populations	High level description of the services and employee populations to be supported
[Subject Matter] Requirements	Description of the specific services to be provided to support the particular function being outsourced
Data, Reports, and Interfaces	Description of the required reports and interfaces necessary to support the services
Compliance Services	Description of the compliance and government reporting services
Service Center	Description of the services to be provided to employees via self-service or the customer service center
Internet Services	Detailed description of the services to be provided via the Internet
Employee Communications	Description of the services required to produce, print, fulfill and distribute materials to employees
Implementation Services	Description of the services to be provided as part of the implementation
Miscellaneous Services	Description of other miscellaneous services required to support the services (e.g. records retention, disaster recovery)
Ad Hoc Services	Description of other required services that may not be "in scope" but that must be supported by the vendor as a change order activity

IDENTIFYING SPECIFIC ELEMENTS AND DOCUMENTING REQUIREMENTS

The next step is to define the specific elements for each dimension of the services identified. The objective of this definitional process is to create a document, the service delivery model, that provides a useful description of the required services at a level of detail sufficient to ensure a common understanding of the vendor's requirements. The simplest way to describe the appropriate level of detail is to keep in mind that you absolutely must describe *what* needs to be done but not *how* to do it. This distinction is important in outsourcing because the *how* is usually related to the systems and staff people who are performing the service. The vendor may perform the same service that your company did itself, using a different and (one hopes) more efficient approach.

The number of specific elements to be defined varies with the scope and complexity of the services being outsourced. Following is a list of the kinds of activities that should be included in the service delivery model:

- Individual employee transactions

- Scheduled processes and procedures

- Periodic batch processes

- Specific deliverables, such as reports, interface files, and government filings

Then, for each specific element that is identified, you need to document your expectations regarding the roles that your organization, the vendor, and any third-party providers will play in delivering the services. In addition, where applicable, these requirements should

Table 4.2

Sample Requirements for the Health & Welfare Enrollment Process

CLIENT RESPONSIBILITY	VENDOR RESPONSIBILITY	THIRD-PARTY RESPONSIBILITY	PERFORMANCE EXPECTATION
• Accept payroll instructions from vendor via periodic payroll file • Initiate payroll deductions	• Accept enrollment elections via Service Center • Review / approve evidence of insurability • Mail confirmation statement • Transmit enrollment instructions to carriers	• Edit PCP elections • Mail cards or other specific correspondence	• Post elections and mail confirmation statement within 2 business days of receipt • Provide instructions to payroll within 5 business days of enrollment • Provide instructions to carrier on next scheduled feed

include performance expectations for each aspect of the work. Table 4.2 illustrates a sample requirement for the enrollment process under a health and welfare plan.

Note: When defining your requirements, remember to reflect the future state. In other words, you are documenting the postoutsourcing roles and responsibilities and performance expectations—not the current responsibilities and turnaround times.

DEFINING YOUR PERFORMANCE EXPECTATIONS

Clearly defining performance expectations is as important as describing the services that are required. Consider paycheck distribution, a process within payroll administration, as an example. Providing paychecks three days late would satisfy the requirement of distributing paychecks each month. It is only the addition of the performance expectation that paychecks be distributed on or before the last day of the month that completes the accurate requirement for successful paycheck distribution.

We've already shown how to capture your performance expectations for each aspect of the services in the previous section. Doing so is the first step in establishing an overall framework for the monitoring of the quality of services with your vendor. The one disadvantage of the approach described above is that it results in too many performance metrics to be practical to manage or may even require the vendor to acknowledge a general expectation that it is unable to measure automatically.

As a result, most outsourcing arrangements also develop a *service level agreement*, which tends to complement the service delivery model as another attachment to the contract. A service level agreement is a subset of the overall set of performance expectations that will be measured and reported by the vendor on a regular basis. The vendor's ability to meet the agreed-upon service levels contained in the service level agreement will form the basis for the objective evaluation of whether the vendor's performance is acceptable.

Performance Penalties and Incentives

One option is to associate financial incentives, called *performance penalties*, with the service levels as a method for providing an incentive for the vendor to achieve quality objectives. Defining the appropriate service levels for an outsourcing relationship can vary depending on the maturity of the outsourcing marketplace or the specific needs of the organization. It is also important not to place too much emphasis on the use of financial penalties to achieve service objectives. Chapter 16 provides a more detailed discussion of the role that performance measurements and penalties play in the management of an outsourcing relationship.

Table 4.3 illustrates a framework for the design and establishment of performance penalties. As shown, the highest level of service is the *performance expectation*—that is, the level of service that is recognized as the buyer's objective. The next level of service is the *performance threshold*. The performance threshold is the level of service below which performance penalties may begin to accrue. Sometimes it makes sense to allow for a neutral zone of performance below the level of expectation but above the performance threshold. The purpose of this neutral zone is to acknowledge that performance is substandard, yet it may not truly be perceived as such by the users of the service. A good example of such a standard might be Internet systems availability. The

Table 4.3
Theoretical Model for Performance Penalties

Performance Level	Example	Rationale
Performance Expectation, as defined in the Service Delivery Model	Internet services available 100% of time 24x7	Agreed upon expectation between the buyer and the vendor
Performance Threshold	Internet services available 98% of expected time	Level of service degradation before service failures begin to adversely impact the perception of the services
Performance Penalty	Payable if Internet services are available less than 98% of expected time	Modest financial penalty to create incentive for vendor to bring its services back into alignment with performance expectations
Maximum Penalty	Payable if Internet services are available less than 90% of expected time	Level at which performance has now degraded beyond acceptable levels. Vendor may be in breach of agreement

performance expectation for availability might be 100 percent of the time, 24 hours per day, 365 days per year. Yet if actual experience was 99 percent, performance may not have meaningfully suffered to the extent a financial penalty is reasonable.

Service Level Agreement Framework

This same theoretical model can be applied across the various dimensions of quality in an outsourcing relationship. It is usually most effective to take a consumer's viewpoint when establishing service levels, although certain service levels may also be appropriate from a sponsor's viewpoint. Table 4.4 provides you with a detailed framework for a comprehensive service level agreement that reflects the multiple dimensions of quality that are implicit in an outsourcing arrangement.

Table 4.4
Framework for a Service Level Agreement

Dimension of Quality	Description
Availability	This dimension of quality ensures that the vendor makes the services reasonably available. These standards are most effective for ensuring that the vendor responds quickly to problems within its systems or telecommunications environment.
Accessibility	This dimension of quality ensures that the vendor is reasonably accessible to users of the service via all available channels (e.g. Internet, voice response, customer service center, email, etc.).
Timeliness	These standards ensure that the vendor is meeting performance expectations for turnaround times on individual user-initiated transactions as well as on scheduled batch activities.
Accuracy	These standards ensure that the vendors work is accurately calculated and communicated to employees.
Employee Satisfaction	This is a subjective standard that provides input with respect to the experience of the users of the services.
Client Satisfaction	This is a subjective standard that provides input with respect to the experience of the sponsor of the services.

Using a multidimensional framework, as illustrated in Table 4.4, provides a balanced scorecard approach to monitoring service levels provided by your vendor. In addition, gathering some subjective data from users and sponsors will allow you to calibrate whether the objective measures are truly reflective of the vendor's perceived performance. Measuring the trend of employee and client satisfaction over time can provide additional insight into whether employee and client perception of the vendor's performance is improving or declining. Chapter 18 provides more information about using a service level agreement to assist in managing a vendor's performance.

Sample Service Level Agreement

Now it is time to put all of these concepts together into practice. Box 4.1 illustrates a sample service level agreement for a benefits administration outsourcing relationship. The service level agreement specifies the purpose of the performance standards, the frequency with which they will be measured and reported, the manner in which the penalties will be calculated, and the limitations, if any, that will be applied to the financial penalties.

Figure 4.1

Service Level Agreement–Benefits Administration

Performance Standard	Description	Penalty
Service Center Availability	Three separate measures:	Calculated as:
	(1) Service center is open 99% of the scheduled time (defined as able to accept phone calls and process transactions)	0.1% for each 1% below 99% for each of the three measures
		Maximum at Risk: [2%]
	(2) IVR is available 99% of the scheduled time (defined as fully functional)	
	(3) Internet available 99% of the scheduled time (defined as fully functional)	
Call Handling	Three separate measures:	Calculated as:
	(1) IVR Availability: 100% of calls reach IVR without a busy signal	0.25% for each 1% below 100%, plus
	(2) CSR Availability: 90% of calls reach a service center representative within 20 seconds	0.2% for each 1% below 90%, plus
		0.1% for each 1% above 3%.
	(3) Abandonment Rate: Fewer than 3% of callers abandon after 20 seconds and prior to reaching a representative	Maximum at Risk: [2%]

Figure 4.1
Service Level Agreement–Benefits Administration (Continued)

Performance Standard	Description	Penalty
Case Management	Three separate measures: (1) 95% of cases are resolved within 5 business days of being opened* (2) 98% of cases are resolved within 10 business days of being opened* (3) 100% of cases are resolved within 20 business days of being opened* * Excluding work activities and cases pended for participant or actions	Calculated as: 0.1% for each 1% below 95% within 5 business days, plus 0.25% for each 1% below 98% within 10 business days, plus 0.5% for each 1% below 100% within 20 business days. Maximum at Risk: [3%]
Work Activities	A single measure that considers the following areas: 90% of activities to be measured delivered timely per the Performance Expectations contained within the Service Delivery Model The activities to be measured are: *Defined Benefit:* • Pension estimate requests • Retirement kit production • Retirement initiations • Survivor processing • QDRO qualifications *Health & Welfare:* • New hire kit production • QMSCO qualifications • COBRA notifications *Defined Contribution:* • New loans • Hardship withdrawals • In-service withdrawals • Distribution commencements • QDRO qualifications	Calculated as: 0.25% for each 1% below 90%. Maximum at Risk: [2%]

Figure 4.1 continues

Figure 4.1
Service Level Agreement–Benefits Administration (Continued)

Performance Standard	Description	Penalty
Production Timeliness	Three separate measures:	Calculated as:
	(1) No more than 2 HR data files posted outside of 1 business day of receipt each month	0.5% for each HR data file above 2 posted outside of 1 business day, plus
	(2) 100% of payroll files posted within 1 business day of receipt of file and assets	1.0% for each payroll file posted outside of 1 business day
	(3) 100% of carrier eligibility files transmitted according to production schedule	1.0% for each carrier file not transmitted according to schedule
		Maximum at Risk: [3%]
Production Accuracy	Two separate measures:	Calculated as:
	(1) 1% of automated participant communications audited with 99.9% accuracy	0.5% for each 1% below 99%, plus
	(2) 10% of manual processes audited with 95% accuracy	0.5% s for each 1% below 95%
		Maximum at Risk: [2%]
Participant Satisfaction	Two measures:	Calculated as:
	(1) 90% of surveyed participants answer "good" or higher on a five-point scale	0.10% for each 1% below 90%, plus
	(2) 80% of surveyed participants answer "very good" or "excellent" on a five-point scale	0.05% for each 1% below 80%
		Maximum at Risk: [2%]

CHAPTER 5

Identifying and Prequalifying Vendors

There are many providers of HR outsourcing services in the marketplace today. This chapter explores the methods that can be used to distinguish among the potential alternatives that appear to be available at first glance. The objective is to refine the search for a provider to a manageable number of organizations that can be considered as part of the outsourcing selection process.

Identifying Types of Outsourcing Vendors

A first step is to distinguish among the universe of potential service providers. Table 5.1 lists the types of organizations within the vendor community, along with a description of their high-level value proposition for clients.

Table 5.1 can be used as an initial filter by identifying the value proposition that is most closely aligned with your organization's outsourcing needs. Identifying the various value propositions available in the marketplace will help you understand how vendors with very different services can describe themselves in a similar way. Such an understanding will help you make an effective decision about which vendors to include in your process.

Table 5.1

Types of Human Resources Providers

Type	Description	Value Proposition
Software application developers	Technology firms that seek to develop software applications that can be sold to HR organizations to provide solutions for specific needs	Leverage the development of a solution that can be used by multiple clients, allowing a reasonable level of customization Provide a traditional alternative solution to internal development Are often a precursor to the emergence of outstanding alternatives
Application service providers	Technology-based firms that not only implement customized software, but also maintain and operate the software on their own computer systems on behalf of the client organization	Seek to further leverage their software applications by providing scalable expert resources for the application's operation, support, maintenance, and enhancement
Consulting firms	Professional service firms that are oriented toward providing expert advice and counsel to clients regarding the technical aspects of HR (These firms can be local, regional, national, or international organizations.)	Leverage their depth or breadth of expertise across multiple clients Desire to provide a full suite of services to their clients so that they can become their preferred partner for HR solutions Are an excellent source for highly customized solutions
Third-party administrators	Typically local or regional providers of HR administration services to small- to medium-sized organizations	Perform largely manual HR administration using resources that can be shared among multiple clients to reduce cost or to increase access to knowledgeable professionals
Specialist outsourcing providers	Companies that specialize in one specific subprocess within HR and that provide a full outsourcing solution for a particularly difficult and complex subprocess within HR (Examples might include COBRA administration, qualified domestic relations order administration, or payroll tax withholding and reporting.)	Solve a particularly difficult aspect of HR that requires a high level of technical expertise or very specialized resources or that has significant legal or operational consequences for its incorrect performance
Insurance carriers	Firms that provide an integrated administrative and benefit program offering in support of health and welfare programs, such as medical, life insurance, or disability benefits	Provide a market-competitive level of benefits in conjunction with an acceptable level of service

Table 5.1

Types of Human Resources Providers (Continued)

Type	Description	Value Proposition
HR outsourcing providers	Administrative services firms that are organized to provide both software and services required to perform a least one entire HR process on behalf of their clients	Provide a holistic approach that allows the client to shift primary responsibility to the provider and to potentially avoid future investments in compliance or service enhancement
Business process outsourcing providers	Global administrative service providers that can provide services across a variety of internal functions, including not only HR but also finance, IT, and so forth	Provide the opportunity for midsize organizations to create greater scale or for organizations interested in shared services beyond HR Often have more experience with global services

Probing Vendor Solutions

There are thousands of providers of HR outsourcing services. However, usually only a handful of providers will match the specific set of requirements for your organization. The trick is to understand the characteristics of both your organization and your outsourcing needs that make your situation unique. Table 5.2 lists the key factors that distinguish vendors in the marketplace.

Before embarking on a search to identify potential providers, you should consider the characteristics of the support you are seeking, using Table 5.2 as a guide. For example, if your organization is a large one, with 10,000 employees nationally, and if you need a health and welfare administration provider, you can quickly go through this list and see that you are looking for the following key features in potential vendors:

- A vendor that provides outsourcing services, not a health and welfare software application that your organization must install

- A vendor that provides administrative support, not a medical or life insurance carrier that wants to supply your plan benefits

- A vendor that serves large companies nationally, not a local or regional third-party administrator

- A vendor that provides end-to-end solutions, not a COBRA or flexible spending account administrator

- A vendor that primarily supports U.S. domestic services, not an organization that focuses on international requirements

Table 5.2

Third-Party Provider Distinguishing Factors

Factor	Description	Examples
Software or services	Many providers sell software for internal installation rather than support outsourced services.	Oracle or SAP for the HR information system
Benefits or services	Some providers really seek to provide plan or program benefits and to provide only administration services as minimally required.	Medical, life, or disability insurance carriers Domestic relocation service providers Corporate gifts and service award providers
Size of organization	Nearly all providers have aligned their value proposition toward one specific segment of target clients, typically based on the size of the organization.	Small market: 1-1,000 employees Midmarket: 1,000-8,000 employees Large market: 8,000 employees and up
Target market	Most providers have aligned their service offerings with a specific target market.	Local, regional, or national employers Type of employer, such as corporations or governments
Breadth of capabilities	Many providers' solutions are oriented toward solving a specific aspect of HR administration. A few providers offer end-to-end solutions.	Specific solutions: COBRA administration, tax reporting, and application tracking End-to-end solutions: Payroll administration and 401(k) administration
International requirements	Many providers offer either a U.S.-only or a North American set of services. A few providers offer international services.	Benefits or payroll administration vary by country because of differences in local laws.

Identifying Potential Providers

Once an organization has identified its own key distinguishing factors, it can finally begin to research the provider community by looking for vendors with similar characteristics. There are several methods for researching outsourcing providers:

1. Reviewing industry listings published in the major HR periodicals such as *HRO World, Employee Benefit News,* or *Human Resources Executive*

2. Reviewing industry listings published by various HR organizations such as the Society for Human Resource Management (SHRM) or the Conference Board

3. Asking peer organizations for recommendations

4. Asking consulting advisors for recommendations

5. Conducting direct research on the Internet through keyword searches

Most organizations use some combination of those approaches to identify potential providers for an internally managed sourcing process. However, if your organization is using a sourcing advisor to assist in the management of the process, that advisor should have a working knowledge of the correct provider community for consideration in the process.

Researching Providers on the Internet

Although the Internet has made it easier to find potential providers, it has also made it more difficult to distinguish among the providers. Any organization can make a reasonable investment in a Web site to create what can appear to be a robust set of capabilities across a broad spectrum of service areas. Here are some helpful hints for refining the search criteria:

- Start big and then refine to small.

- Use industry sources for initial lists of potential organizations.

- Identify keywords that can be combined with more generic terms to refine your search criteria. For example, you might use the keyword *content* in conjunction with the generic term *learning*

- Look at the relative volume of information on a provider's Web site about the specific area that you are searching. For example, a provider with thirty pages on payroll and two pages on learning is less likely to be a leading learning content provider.

- Once you have identified a number of potential providers, search their sites for characteristics for characteristics that match those of your company, as identified using Tables 5.1 and 5.2.

Prequalifying Potential Providers

Note that it is important not only to identify potential providers, but also to prequalify them in some fashion for your sourcing process. A common mistake that many organizations make is to assume that it is good practice to include a long list of providers in the sourcing process and then to use the results of their proposal responses to determine which providers deserve additional scrutiny.

Prequalifying vendors is the best approach to take in an outsourcing process for several reasons. First, it is expensive and time-consuming for providers to respond to RFPs. Therefore, they will appreciate having a reasonable opportunity to win the assignment rather than merely being included as a courtesy. Second, it is much more time-consuming to review provider proposals than may be apparent when the RFPs are distributed. Therefore, it is usually more valuable to spend quality time reviewing a proposal from a vendor that you are relatively certain can satisfy your criteria rather than reading additional RFP responses from vendors that are marginally positioned to satisfy your requirements.

An additional complication in the prequalification of providers that needs to be considered is the importance of any preexisting relationships. For example, a provider may supply related services to your finance department, such as trust services, or it may supply consulting services to your IT department. In such instances, it is important to explicitly review each provider against a set of criteria to determine whether the provider should be included in or excluded from the remainder of the process. If you exclude a provider with an existing relationship with your organization, it is usually worthwhile to review the decision with the functional owner of the relationship within your organization. Apprising that individual of the reason for the exclusion in advance of the RFP being distributed will reduce the probability of a provider being added to the process in midstream—a practice that not only can be disruptive to your schedule, but also can diminish the perceived integrity of your process both internally and externally.

Using a Request for Information

The optimal number of recipients for any RFP for outsourcing services is somewhere between four and eight organizations. However, sometimes at the end of a provider identification and prequalification process, a larger number of providers will appear to be qualified. If so, you may want to consider issuing a short request for information (RFI) to this larger group of providers.

The purpose of an RFI is to gather additional information that can be used to distinguish the relevant capabilities of the providers. You can use this information to complete the vendor prequalification process. A common mistake is to issue a mini-RFP in the form of an RFI. This approach merely gathers more general information that can be equally confusing when trying to distinguish among a set of providers. We recommend using the RFI to capture specific, objective data about the firm and its direct experience with similar assignments. You might think of the RFI as gathering the data that would normally be collected as part of the company profile section of the RFP, as described in Chapter 6. These data can, in most cases, be used to form the basis of your selecting the RFP recipients. A sample RFI that is designed to gather simple factual information from a set of vendors for making such a determination has been included the accompanying CD-ROM.

CHAPTER 6

Preparing and Analyzing a Request for Proposal

In Chapter 4, we described the process for defining your outsourcing requirements. In Chapter 5, we shared how to identify and prequalify an appropriate set of potential vendors. The next two chapters provide a more detailed description of how to manage the vendor selection process that was introduced in Chapter 3. In this chapter, we answer the following questions:

- How do you establish vendor selection criteria?

- How do you prepare a request for proposal?

- How do you distribute the RFP?

- How should you support the vendors as they draft their proposals?

Establishing Your Selection Criteria

In Chapter 3, we discussed how important it was to establish the organization's goals for the outsourcing project. In particular, we emphasized the need to understand the relative importance of things such as the cost savings when compared with access to new technology or the quality of service when compared with the desire to have a scalable infrastructure. Those goals will now begin to get reflected explicitly in the criteria you establish to evaluate potential vendors.

There is an art to establishing vendor selection criteria. If you are not careful, you will end up with a long list of items that are important to the selection process. The result of having too long a list is that none of the criteria end up being important. For example, if you establish twenty criteria upon which to make the vendor selection, then no one criterion will have more than a 5 to 10 percent influence on the final decision.

It is best to limit the number of selection criteria to no more than ten. All of the items that you have identified as important should be mapped within those higher-level criteria. Limiting the number of criteria will force you to differentiate strategic decision-making factors from specific areas of concern.

You may want to develop two sets of selection criteria: an initial set of criteria for evaluating the vendor proposals and a second set of criteria for selecting the recommended vendor from among the finalists. Many clients decrease the weighting of cost in the initial evaluations or may eliminate the weighting for an item such as the company's profile once the vendors have established their credibility. Table 6.1 illustrates ten common criteria that can be used in the vendor selection process, along with an example of how the weightings might reasonably change between the initial proposal analysis and the final vendor selection.

Table 6.1

Sample Vendor Selection Criteria and Weightings

Selection Criteria	Proposal Analysis Weighting (%)	Finalist Analysis Weighting (%)
Company profile and business stability	10	0
Account and relationship management	10	10
Customer service	10	10
Systems and technology	15	20
Administrative expertise: service area 1	15	10
Administrative expertise: service area 2	15	10
Administrative expertise: service area 3	15	10
Implementation and transition expertise	10	10
Contract terms and conditions	0	5
Fees	0	15
Total	**100**	**100%**

In the example in Table 6.1, some weight is given to the stability of the organizations being considered as finalists, but once that decision is reached, that criterion is no longer considered a distinguishing factor among finalists. Similarly, higher emphasis might be placed on demonstrated ability to satisfy the specific service area requirements during the proposal phase, but once finalists are identified, the differentiating factors are more likely to be found in the systems and technology area; hence, you may find it appropriate to shift more emphasis to that category during the evaluation of finalists.

Note: It is a good idea to establish the proposal analysis weighting before you receive the proposals. Similarly, you should determine the finalist analysis weighting before performing due diligence.

Handling Fees in the Selection Criteria

Two different approaches are commonly used for balancing vendors' fee proposals within the selection criteria framework:

1. Explicitly include fees in the overall criteria as illustrated above.

2. Exclude fees from the selection criteria and account for them separately.

Most organizations use a combination of these approaches. They exclude fees from the analysis of the original proposals and then incorporate fees explicitly in the comparison of finalists, as illustrated in Figure 6.1. Key contract terms should also be included explicitly in the overall analysis of the providers, particularly terms that affect the value of the fee proposals. Remember, one of the three characteristics of an outsourcing relationship is that it can be captured in a mutually acceptable contractual agreement (see Chapter 1). Therefore, it is always useful to keep that ultimate goal front and center during a vendor selection process.

Furthermore, to arrive at a selection, you must explicitly or implicitly evaluate the relative importance of the financial relationship. In other words, fees will need to be balanced against other selection criteria as part of making your final decision. In our experience, it is more difficult to balance fees against the other criteria if they are not being modeled explicitly, so we generally recommend handling fees in the manner we have described.

Structuring the Request for Proposals

An RFP needs to accomplish the following objectives:

- Define the process and timeline that your organization is going to follow in selecting the vendor.

- Provide the vendors with your business outsourcing requirements and with a formal opportunity to allow them to ask clarifying questions.

- Provide the vendors with sufficient information to enable them to provide an actionable fee proposal.

- Secure information about the vendors' capabilities that will assist you in evaluating their proposals.

- Protect your organization's legal interests in the process while maintaining maximum flexibility to reach your decision.

Your goal when drafting an RFP should be to communicate as effectively as possible so that you can secure the best proposals available from the marketplace. A poorly drafted RFP will usually result in poor proposal responses. The vendors may conclude that your organization is not serious about the engagement or that your organization will be difficult to do business with. Or if the RFP does not contain sufficient information about your requirements or your company, the vendors will typically place caveats on their fee and service proposal. Those caveats will inhibit your ability to contrast and compare the responses you receive.

In addition, you should remember that you are providing the vendors with a reasonably short timeframe within which to (a) distribute your proposal internally; (b) identify a team to respond; (c) assimilate your business requirements; (d) draft their responses; and (e) write, print, assemble, and produce multiple copies of their response. The more efficiently your RFP communicates your requirements, the better the responses you are likely to receive.

Integrating Your Vendor Selection and Contracting Processes

It is essential to remember that a vendor selection process results in a contract with the successful provider. One of the most common mistakes companies make when outsourcing is to separate the selection and contracting processes. It is critical that the vendor selection process be integrated with the contracting process to ensure that the outsourcing relationship is captured as it was described during the selection process.

This integrated relationship between the proposal and contracting processes is illustrated in Figure 6.1. As shown in the figure, the RFP should be designed to establish the following:

- The services the vendor will provide (described in the form of a service delivery model)

- The performance expectations for the services

- The volume of services required

Figure 6.1
Integration between RFP and Contract

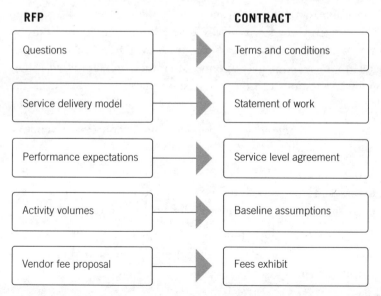

In addition, it is possible to ask questions in the RFP about the vendor's willingness to comply with your key contract terms and conditions.

In response to the RFP, the vendor should not only indicate its ability to satisfy your requirements but also provide the final element of the contract—what fees will be paid in exchange for the services. By structuring the RFP as illustrated above, you have begun the process of negotiating your agreement with the successful vendor as part of the vendor selection process. This approach will minimize the likelihood of misunderstandings between your organization and the successful vendor.

Probing for Vendor Capabilities

In Chapter 4, we described in detail the process for drafting a service delivery model as well as a set of performance expectations or even a service level agreement. The other major section contained in the RFP is one that contains questions designed to help you understand the vendors' capabilities and their proposed solutions to your requirements.

Some thought should be given to the inclusion of questions in your RFP. It is too easy to add whatever questions come to mind to ask the vendors. However, vendors typically have a limited amount of time to respond to an RFP. Moreover, your team will have only so much capacity for reviewing the responses after they are submitted. Thus, asking fewer questions will typically result in better proposals from the vendors and more time for analysis by your team.

When drafting potential questions for submission to the vendors, consider the following:

- Avoid questions designed to determine whether the vendor understands the work you do. Such questions should already have been answered as part of the vendor prequalification process.

- Ask some high-level, free-form questions that will allow the vendors to articulate their value propositions and their distinguishing characteristics.

When reviewing potential questions for submission to the vendors, evaluate the following:

- Will the question elicit objective factual information that can be compared among vendors?

- Is the question better suited for on-site due diligence later in the process rather than inclusion at the RFP stage?

- Can a single question represent two or three similar questions?

Following those simple steps will improve the quality of both the RFP and the vendor proposals.

Requesting Fee Proposals

The other part of the RFP that needs some specific structure is the section that asks the vendors to provide their fee proposal. First, it is important to structure this section to ensure that you will receive an actionable fee proposal, not just an estimate of the vendor's proposed fees. We recommend a clear statement in the preamble of this section that indicates the following about the requested fee proposal:

- It must include all of the services required in the service delivery model.

- It recognizes the performance expectations that have been defined.

- It is based on the employee data and other volume assumptions that have been provided in the RFP.

- It is all-inclusive.

The last point is particularly important, because vendors have myriad pricing methodologies. Although your fee request section should attempt to anticipate as many fee approaches as possible, the vendors should be made responsible for ensuring that they have provided a complete and comprehensive fee proposal.

Satisfying Internal Sourcing Requirements

Most large organizations today have certain internal standards for managing a vendor selection process. Your organization may have concerns about ensuring that the vendors treat the information provided in the RFP as proprietary and confidential. Sometimes, vendors are even required to sign separate nondisclosure agreements before becoming eligible to receive an RFP.

In addition, the RFP should specify that the vendors respond at their own volition and cost, that their proposals are binding, that your organization is not making any commitment to purchase services, and that contact between the vendor and your organization should follow prescribed channels. Those provisions are illustrated in the sample RFP found on the accompanying CD-ROM.

Distributing the Request for Proposals

Now it is time to distribute the complete RFP to the vendors for their consideration and response. Give the vendors a minimum of three weeks—preferably four—to produce a good proposal. It will take about one week for the vendors to distribute the RFP internally, one week to develop a strategy for their response, one week to write the proposal, and one week to produce the proposal and conduct internal quality reviews. A longer response timeframe may be appropriate for large assignments. Shortening the response time may have negative consequences, such as receiving proposals that do not demonstrate the vendor's true capabilities or do not respond to your requirements.

Supporting the Vendors as They Develop Their Responses

Keeping in mind that your objective is to secure the vendors' best proposal responses, you should anticipate investing time in supporting the vendors as they develop their proposals. At a minimum, you should be available to respond to specific questions from each vendor through conference calls or email. For large-scale HR outsourcing projects, you may even want to consider holding on-site discovery sessions to allow the vendors to ask detailed questions about your requirements, systems, processes, and procedures.

There are different schools of thought with respect to how structured this process needs to be to maintain equity among the vendors. Some organizations control the method under which questions may be submitted and then provide copies of both the question and the response to all of the vendors. In the end, the amount of control to be exercised is a matter of choice. However, to the extent that any question identifies either a mistake or a lack of clarity in the RFP, it is important to provide additional information to all of the vendors.

Using Technology to Simplify the Process

Some large outsourcing projects require the communication of extensive amounts of information. For example, if your organization is considering outsourcing all of its workforce administration globally, you may want to provide the vendors with access to your entire library of policies and procedures.

Rather than provide this information on paper, which is difficult to produce and inefficient for the vendors to distribute internally, you may want to consider an electronic approach. There are a number of popular Internet providers of content management software. For a reasonable subscription fee, you can establish a secure Web site that the vendors can access to review your materials online. This approach simplifies and facilitates the distribution of documents. The vendors can also post their proposal responses to the same Web site, a feature that can accelerate your own distribution of their responses while simultaneously providing documentation of the history of your exchanges of information.

Finally, there are also software solutions to providing RFPs online that will manage the RFP document itself, control the communications between your organization and the vendors, log the email streams between the organizations, and facilitate the collection of the vendors' proposals. Your sourcing or procurement organizations are likely to be familiar with those services.

Helpful hint: If the vendors will be submitting written proposals, ask them to provide sufficient copies for each member of the vendor selection team.

CHAPTER 7
Analyzing the Request for Proposals, Selecting Finalists, and Making a Decision

Now that the vendor proposals have been received, what do you do next? In this chapter, we will describe how to do the following:

- Analyze the vendor proposals.

- Analyze the fee proposals.

- Select your finalists.

- Perform the due diligence process.

- Identify your preferred vendor.

- Negotiate the best deal for your organization.

Summarizing and Analyzing the Vendor Proposals

The first step is to read and summarize the vendor proposals. The best way to summarize proposal responses is side by side. Most vendors can provide responses electronically, so the simplest method is to combine the various proposals into a single document by cutting and pasting. If time allows, an even better approach is to summarize each vendor's response. This approach requires that you consider all responses and crystallize whether they deliver the information you want. This task can be time-consuming, but the resulting document will be more effective in distinguishing among the vendors' capabilities. In addition, proposal summaries become useful reference documents during the remainder of the selection process.

Once the proposals have been read and summarized, you can begin the analysis. To analyze the proposals, you may want to consider scoring each of the vendor's responses to your questions. The objective of this scoring exercise is to develop an objective assessment of the relative attractiveness of each of the vendor's proposals using some type of mechanism for consistency.

We recommend the following four-point scoring method:

0 = No capabilities or unacceptable response

1 = Inadequate capabilities or inadequate response

3 = Adequate capabilities or adequate response

4 = Superior capabilities or superior response

We have intentionally not included a score of 2 in this scale. The purpose of this skewed method of scoring is twofold. First, it is difficult to differentiate between vendors' capabilities on the basis of an RFP response. Therefore, you should look for vendors to demonstrate that they have the necessary capabilities and should provide extra points only when vendors can add extra value, such as by offering services beyond your requirements like extensive Internet services. Second, it is difficult for vendors to overcome gaps in their service offerings, so the penalty for missing capabilities should be greater than the bonus for exceptional capabilities.

Ideally, the questions section of the RFP was organized in a fashion consistent with the vendor selection criteria. But if not, you can map each of the questions in the RFP into one of the vendor selection criteria at this stage in the process. Generally, each question can be assigned an equal weighting. However, it is also possible to weight the responses to different questions if you believe one is more important than another.

Analyzing Fee Proposals

One of the more difficult aspects of analyzing vendor proposals is to summarize the fee proposals. Vendor fees usually consist of some combination of a relatively short list of common components. Each of those components may require some kind of adjustment in your analysis of the fee proposals, as described in Table 7.1. The net effect of making the adjustments is to normalize the various proposals of the vendors under consideration to improve their comparability. In addition, it is usually also necessary to project the various proposals outward for three to five years to reflect any variations in inflation adjustments among the proposals.

Table 7.1

Normalizing Common Vendor Fee Components

Implementation fee	One-time fee for the transition of the services to the vendor	Try to ensure that this fee is fixed and is not subject to reevaluation after requirements are completed.
Fixed fee	Base annual fee for services expressed either as a monthly fixed dollar amount or on a per employee per month basis	Try to ensure that the fee is all-inclusive.
Scope limitation	An indication by the vendor that it has limited the "in scope" services to some amount of volume that was not specified in the RFP (e.g., number of hours of ad hoc reporting support)	Possibly make an adjustment to the vendor's proposal to ensure consistency among all of the vendor responses.
Volume fee	A fee that varies with the amount of use of some aspect of the vendor's environment (e.g., the number of call minutes into the customer service function)	Make an adjustment to the vendor's proposal that is based on a reasonable and consistent estimate of the volume of activity that is likely to be incurred.
Transaction fee	A fee that varies with the number of specific transactions that occur (e.g., a qualified domestic relations order qualification fee)	Make an adjustment to the vendor's proposal that is based on a reasonable estimate of the expected transaction volume.
Employee or participant fee	A fee-often a transaction-based fee- that is payable by the employee or plan participant and not by the employer or plan sponsor (e.g., a loan setup fee in a 401k plan)	Make an adjustment to calculate the annual value of these fees and to add it to the vendor's proposal. The allocation of cost between the employer and employees should be a strategic decision, not a vendor's pricing algorithm.

Table 7.1 continues

Table 7.1

Normalizing Common Vendor Fee Components (Continued)

Pass-through expenses	Expenses that most commonly include travel, postage and shipping, and telecommunications	Possibly try to ensure that travel expenses are consistent with your internal travel policy guidelines.
		Possibly request that the vendor provide you with a reasonable estimate of the annual expenses for each category.
Subsidies	Subsidies that some vendors are able to provide to their fees through either asset management fees or "float" on cash payments (e.g., in payroll administration).	Require vendor to provide explicit data, because subsidies are the most difficult adjustments to make.

There is no shortcut for reviewing fee proposals. Instead, you must do a careful and detailed review of each vendor's fee proposal on a line-by-line basis. You may need to contact the vendor to clarify certain aspects of the fee proposal or to understand any assumptions the vendor may have made. Sometimes, to ensure the comparability of the proposals, you may even need to go back to the other vendors to ask them to revise their fee proposals to accommodate the assumptions made by one vendor.

Selecting Finalists

Once you have completed the fee and service proposal analysis, it is time to select the finalists. The optimal number of finalist organizations is three. Three finalists will provide your vendor selection team with a good basis for comparability of the solutions during the due diligence process. Sometimes more or fewer vendors may be appropriate, but three is always a good number to use as a target.

The process for identifying finalists is to work through an objective evaluation of the proposals. On the basis of the summaries you have produced, each member of the vendor selection team should reach his or her own preliminary assessment of each vendor's proposal. Then, the entire team can gather to discuss the vendor proposals and how each member of the team personally evaluated them. Often, different team members will have reached different conclusions, and the open discussion of team members' observations will improve the entire team's understanding of the proposals. Throughout this team discussion, members should be allowed to revise their scores. At the end of the meeting, the scores can be tabulated, and a preliminary slate of finalist organizations can be identified that is based purely on the scoring.

At this step, it is often useful to take into account other factors, such as a preexisting relationship or a deal-breaking weakness that may have been observed in an otherwise acceptable proposal. Remember, the objective of the entire vendor selection process is to continue to reduce the list of providers until you find the best match for your organization. Therefore, it is a mistake to allow the process to entirely dictate the results at each step along the way. Instead, the process should provide a framework to facilitate the team's decision making at each step.

At times, you may find that your team is unable to reach consensus on where to make the cutoff for finalists. In that case, it may be effective to go back to the vendors for clarification or for amplification of some of their responses to further differentiate them from the other competitors. Although performing rigorous due diligence on three vendors is a manageable process, the difficulty of maintaining the quality of your due diligence process increases exponentially as you try to include additional finalist organizations. Therefore, whatever it takes, it will be worthwhile to select your finalists at this stage rather than just continuing to evaluate more vendors.

Refining Your Selection Criteria

The entire vendor selection process tends to be an education for the selection team members. Sometimes, the team may be pleasantly surprised by what it learns about the vendors' capabilities to perform the services. For example, your selection team may be concerned most that the vendors can perform the services as effectively as they are currently being performed; therefore, administrative expertise may have had the highest weighting during the proposal analysis phase. But if during that analysis it becomes clear that your finalists all have more experience than you had expected, your team might reasonably conclude that either fees or technology are a more distinguishing factor in the selection of a preferred provider. Such discoveries should be reflected in your selection criteria, as was described in Chapter 6, when you move into the final phase of the selection process.

Performing Due Diligence

Despite all of the effort that goes into constructing a good RFP and analyzing the vendors' written proposals, it is important to perform additional due diligence before you select an outsourcing vendor. The most common method for performing due diligence is to perform site visits. In a site visit, a due diligence team goes on site to the vendor's location to meet the vendor and to observe the work being performed. Most organizations find it useful to see the vendor's facilities and to meet the people they will be working with.

Your efforts to prepare for vendor site visits can help ensure that useful information is gathered for reaching a selection decision. In preparation for a site visit, you should provide each vendor with guidance about what you want to observe. For example, you might want a vendor to clarify certain aspects of its proposal or to explore particular areas of concern.

Your site visit preparation may also be enhanced by performing some reference checks in advance. Reference checking is another form of due diligence, because it provides an opportunity to gather performance evaluation data from the provider's current clients. Reference checks often yield information that can be useful in the site visits by preparing the due diligence team with some insights into each provider's strengths and weaknesses, which can be explored at the site visit.

You do not need to prescribe an agenda that all vendors must follow. Forcing too much structure may inhibit the ability of a vendor to demonstrate what makes its organization unique and why you would want to hire that vendor. However, you should give each vendor some detailed guidelines so that your visit will be successful. In addition, you will want to allocate sufficient time for each site visit to ensure that you can achieve your due diligence objectives.

To assess each site, you can once again use a scoring methodology. Ask your site visit team members to complete their scoring immediately after each visit, while the information is still fresh in their minds; otherwise, site visits tend to blur into one another. However, as the team members complete more site visits, they should feel free to revise their earlier scores as they begin to recognize differences in the vendors' strengths and weaknesses.

Identifying Your Preferred Provider

After completing the site visits, your site visit team can tally its scores. Then, team members should hold a joint meeting or conference call to review the scoring and discuss why each member scored each visit as he or she did. Often, one team member will have observed something that others missed, or sometimes one will have misunderstood what a vendor said. This discussion will refine the scoring process and equip all team members to support the resulting recommendation. With scoring complete, you can apply the vendor selection criteria weightings to the scoring to determine the ordinal ranking of the finalists. Often, the team will have reached a relatively clear consensus on its preferred vendor at this juncture. If not, some level of additional due diligence may be required, as described in the following section.

Negotiating the Best Deal for Your Organization

Selecting an outsourcing provider is like selling a house or getting a new job. If you don't like the offer that has been extended, you should modify it and provide a counterproposal. At this stage in the process, your preferred vendor will be highly motivated to make modest alterations in order to close the deal. It is a common mistake to assume that any loose ends can be cleaned up to your satisfaction during the contracting process. Instead, all loose ends should be cleaned up before the final selection decision is communicated. Enough surprises will arise during contracting without starting the process with a list of changes.

For example, let's assume that your vendor selection decision is down to two providers, Vendor A and Vendor B. Perhaps Vendor A's fee proposal is 15 percent lower than Vendor B's, but you really like some of the functionality contained in Vendor B's systems applications. Thus, you feel vaguely disappointed with both proposals and are having a difficult time making a decision. You can simplify your decision by approaching both vendors and asking them to close the gap. Ask Vendor A if it is willing to add the desired functionality to its systems without increasing its costs. Or ask Vendor B if it is willing to match the pricing of its competitor. In most cases, you'll find both vendors willing to make additional commitments to secure the business. However, you should be prepared for this request to be associated with your commitment to award a vendor the business if it meets your request. Therefore, ideally your team would identify its preferred vendor and the specific improvements that the vendor needs to make to its proposal to secure its selection as the recommended provider.

CHAPTER 8
Communicating the Decision

Taking a Strategic Approach to Outsourcing Communications

The old adage "no news is good news" is absolutely the wrong approach for a company to take as it moves forward with its outsourcing decision. The consequences of little (or no) communications will have a negative impact on all employees—both those whose jobs will be outsourced and those who will remain. Lack of communication will also have a strong effect on non-HR employees and managers, who may be asked to take on new responsibilities and to interact with outsourcing vendors. Be clear on what is being outsourced and what is not, and be certain you understand how the outsourcing plan will affect all employees and all levels of management. Adapt the communications for each audience of stakeholders, reflecting their individual perspective and concerns about the ramifications of the change. Putting the outsourcing decision in perspective can help counter some of the pessimism that might occur. In an overanxious environment, clarity becomes crucial. Communicating the facts is not enough. You must anticipate and dispel potential rumors as well.

Communicating the Positives and the Negatives

When you are looking at methods for communicating the positive side of what employees could view as a negative message, an overly enthusiastic approach isn't the answer. After the downsizings of the 1990s and early 2000s, workers are painfully aware that organizations pursue courses of action that positively affect their bottom line, and those decisions are not necessarily ones that employees want to hear.

Discuss with management the effect the outsourcing decision will have on all of your employees from a strategic perspective. Communications should be clear about what is being outsourced, what will happen to employees currently working in the outsourced function, and how the remaining employees will be affected. Target communications to each of the different audiences: employees to be outsourced, employees who will remain, company department heads, and managers. The decision will affect each of those groups differently, and you want to design communications to reflect those differences.

Outsourcing frequently creates new opportunities for employees who are hired by the vendor. When you're in the process of choosing a vendor, one of the important issues in the negotiations may be whether that company will hire your employees. If the vendor is interested in hiring your employees, you should ascertain how their pay and benefits will be affected.

If you have negotiated a deal in which some of your outsourced employees will move to the vendor's payroll, you will have a more positive message to communicate. The change will still be traumatic, and you and the vendor need to do everything possible to make the change as painless as it can be for your employees.

If you have employees who will be terminated as a result of their function being outsourced, the communications need to be clear and timely. Such communications should be done both in person by an HR professional and in a written communication that establishes the pay and benefits your employees will receive and the timing of the terminations.

Getting employees to buy into the restructuring process that occurs when you outsource parts of the HR function is difficult because their minds are going to dwell on the fear that any restructuring will take place at the expense of their jobs. There has to be full communication to employees about what is going on. If you have negotiated an agreement in which the outsourced employees will have their same position with the vendor and will not experience a drastic alteration in their pay and benefits, you should convey those facts. Communicate that outsourced employees who will be working for the vendor may have increased career opportunities with the vendor because they will be doing the same job but may be doing it for more than one company.

HR employees who remain will want to know exactly how the change will affect them. Will they have more work? Will they have to work longer hours? Will their pay be affected? Is their job safe? Employees will want to know why and how the decision to outsource was made, and they need to know that it is all right to ask questions and to seek answers to the problems and opportunities that outsourcing will bring about for them. Employees who will not be hired by the vendor but instead will be terminated should be provided as much advance notice as possible and should be given severance benefits and assistance in finding another job. Figure 8.1 provides a strategic approach to communications about outsourcing.

Figure 8.1
A Strategic Approach to Outsourcing Communication

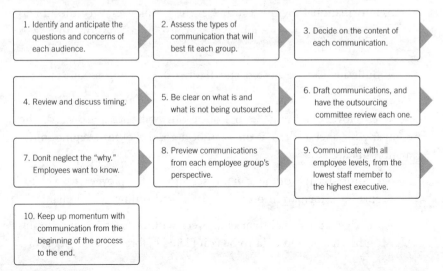

1. Identify and anticipate the questions and concerns of each audience.

2. Assess the types of communication that will best fit each group.

3. Decide on the content of each communication.

4. Review and discuss timing.

5. Be clear on what is and what is not being outsourced.

6. Draft communications, and have the outsourcing committee review each one.

7. Don't neglect the "why." Employees want to know.

8. Preview communications from each employee group's perspective.

9. Communicate with all employee levels, from the lowest staff member to the highest executive.

10. Keep up momentum with communication from the beginning of the process to the end.

Using a "Five Ws" Approach to Communications

When you are ready to tell employees about the outsourcing decision, a simple way to plan the communications is to use a "five Ws" approach:

Why: Why are you outsourcing HR functions?

What: What HR functions will be outsourced? What vendor will be providing the services?

Who: Whose jobs will be outsourced, and will those employees be hired by the vendor? If not, what benefits will be provided to terminated employees?

Where: Where is the vendor located?

When: When will the change occur, and how much time will it take?

Identifying the Methods of Communication

Methods of communication will vary depending on the size of the group to be outsourced. Some communication methods that might be used follow:

1. Individual meetings can be established with each employee.

2. Group meetings work well when a large group is to be outsourced.

3. Informational memos can be sent to employees. Vary the memo for employees whose jobs will be outsourced and for those who will remain.

4. Bulletins can be posted and frequently updated as outsourcing plans progress.

If employees' jobs at several locations will be outsourced, the company intranet, if there is one, can be a good tool for keeping information updated.

6. A short-term hotline can be set up for employees to call for current information on the logistics and timing of the change.

7. Managers can email their employees with instructions and timing of the change and tasks to be completed before the change occurs.

8. Daily voicemail updates can keep employees posted about any changes that arise suddenly.

If the vendor will be hiring your employees on a predetermined date, the vendor should keep the affected employees posted about the timing of the change and should provide information on their jobs, location of their offices, company policies and procedures, pay, and benefits. You can schedule meetings on your premises or at the vendor's offices so that employees get used to an impending move.

Considering Three Communication Scenarios

Consider these three scenarios of communicating with employees.

SCENARIO 1: COMMUNICATE WITH ALL COMPANY EMPLOYEES

The first announcement to be published should be addressed to all employees and should tell them why the decision was made to outsource the HR function (or parts of the function). The announcement should include the vendor's name; a description of the vendor, including (if appropriate) a list of the vendor's other clients; and the timetable for the change. It should also state whether the vendor will be hiring HR employees or whether a reduction in force (RIF) will occur. If a RIF will take place, the timing should be described, as well as the other particulars of any reorganization.

SCENARIO 2: COMMUNICATE WITH EMPLOYEES WHO WILL BE OFFERED JOBS WITH THE VENDOR

Communications should come from both you and the vendor. First, have a meeting with employees to announce your decision and to provide time for questions. Then, send a memo to all affected employees. Your memo to employees who will be outsourced should be sent first and should detail the reasons you're outsourcing. The vendor's letter should follow shortly thereafter.

Example: You have a meeting. Then you send a letter to employees confirming what was said at the meeting and telling them that the vendor will be contacting them about jobs. The vendor prepares a letter offering employees jobs, specifying salary and benefits, and providing dates for acceptance, along with employment applications to be completed and returned.

SCENARIO 3: COMMUNICATE WITH EMPLOYEES WHO WILL BE TERMINATED WITH NO JOB OFFER

No one likes the idea of a RIF, but if you plan to outsource certain HR activities and the vendor you are going to use will not be hiring your employees, you need to make special plans for the termination package that you will give to employees who will be leaving.

Communications should be honest and timely. Employees should be offered a severance package that includes severance pay, assistance with a job search, and paid medical benefits through a specified time period of at least thirty days. Offer as much assistance as the company can afford to help employees find a job quickly and to ease dislocation and fear. Notify other organizations in your area that employees will be available on a specific date.

Example: Some companies offer one-week severance for each year of service, capped at sixteen weeks. A minimum severance may be established at thirty days, so those employees who have a short tenure will not be out of work with only one or two weeks pay. Offer an extension of medical benefits for thirty, sixty, or ninety days, depending on your resources. Provide assistance with resume preparation and job search skills. If you don't have HR professionals on staff who can provide those services, hire an outside consultant. A specific policy should be determined and written before you make any announcement.

Organizations are also required to provide extended insurance benefits under the Consolidated Omnibus Budget Reconciliation Act (COBRA). They are required to provide notification under the Health Insurance Portability and Accountability Act (HIPAA). Employees will be eligible for unemployment compensation insurance as dictated by the laws of the states in which the reductions will occur.

Note: Your HR executive should review the current COBRA and HIPAA regulations to ensure compliance.

Planning for Communications

Effective communications require planning, and any outsourcing initiative will be most effective if the communications are well thought out and targeted to each audience. Employees have become more sophisticated and knowledgeable and want more information today than they required just a few years ago. Supervisors and managers are also more vocal in expressing frustration when company communications are inadequate on issues that are pivotal to their well-being and the well-being of their employees. Outsourcing creates an anxious environment; therefore, timing and clarity are crucial. It is a good idea to use a communication checklist to ensure that all bases are covered. Figure 8.2 is a communication checklist for HR outsourcing.

Figure 8.2
Communication Checklist for HR Outsourcing

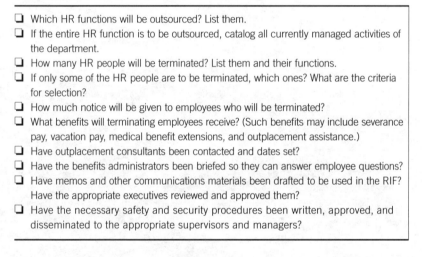

❑ Which HR functions will be outsourced? List them.
❑ If the entire HR function is to be outsourced, catalog all currently managed activities of the department.
❑ How many HR people will be terminated? List them and their functions.
❑ If only some of the HR people are to be terminated, which ones? What are the criteria for selection?
❑ How much notice will be given to employees who will be terminated?
❑ What benefits will terminating employees receive? (Such benefits may include severance pay, vacation pay, medical benefit extensions, and outplacement assistance.)
❑ Have outplacement consultants been contacted and dates set?
❑ Have the benefits administrators been briefed so they can answer employee questions?
❑ Have memos and other communications materials been drafted to be used in the RIF? Have the appropriate executives reviewed and approved them?
❑ Have the necessary safety and security procedures been written, approved, and disseminated to the appropriate supervisors and managers?

PART III

Outsourcing Specific Functions
and Processes

CHAPTER 9
Outsourcing Workforce Administration

The next series of chapters describe the outsourcing of specific functional elements of HR. Although the general methodology described in Parts I and II of this book should be applied to all outsourcing projects, the following chapters are designed to provide an understanding of some of the nuances relative to each function within HR. We will explore some of the differences in the solutions available and the relative maturity of the vendors in each market. Part III will also provide you with a better understanding of which functional areas can be outsourced on a standalone basis as opposed to those services that are more typically combined with other functional areas in some type of bundled basis.

This chapter describes the process of outsourcing workforce administration, which is often considered the foundation on which the outsourcing of many other functional areas depends. In fact, as we will describe in the following chapters, many functional areas within HR do not have standalone outsourcing solutions and can be outsourced only in conjunction with workforce administration.

Definition of Workforce Administration

Workforce administration is an emerging term in the HR lexicon. It refers to the following set of HR functions and activities:

- Development, maintenance, and operation of human resource information systems

- Employee and manager policy and procedure support

- Employee and manager self-service and customer service

- Employee data management and records retention

Other services that are sometimes included in workforce administration include these:

- Leave administration

- Domestic relocation

When the media describe companies that have outsourced HR, they are talking about companies that have outsourced at least workforce administration. Not surprisingly, workforce administration is often outsourced in combination with other services that are built on the basic employee data, such as compensation administration or performance management.

Prevalence of Outsourcing

Workforce administration is today's emerging functional opportunity. The initial outsourcing engagements in this marketplace appeared around 1999. The watershed event in the evolution of workforce administration outsourcing occurred when BP established its landmark HR outsourcing agreement with Exult. Since that time, the percentage of large employers that have adopted outsourcing as their solution for workforce administration has grown steadily. Today, about 8 percent of organizations with 10,000 or more employees outsource workforce administration.

Marketplace Alternatives

Currently, most employers still perform workforce administration internally using a human resource information system application that was purchased and installed by a major software provider, such as Lawson, Oracle, or SAP.

For those organizations that have adopted outsourcing, there are four different solutions available for outsourcing workforce administration:

Application service providers. In this approach, the ASP vendor will host the HRIS application and may even take over responsibility for its maintenance and enhancement according to the client's requirements. Often, ASP relationships have evolved as a result of a broader IT outsourcing relationship with a company like IBM or EDS.

Point solutions. Other organizations have established external customer service functions using their internal HRIS application to provide the employee and manager servicing components of workforce administration under a "point solution" or co-sourcing arrangement. In those relationships, the client is still responsible for the maintenance and enhancement of the underlying HRIS applications, but the vendor provides employee and manager support.

Human resource outsourcing. HRO is sometimes referred to as the transform then transfer approach. Under this alternative, the vendor goes through an implementation and conversion of the client's systems and processing environment to its own processes, systems, and staff. In essence, the existing client environment is replaced by the vendor's environment. The HRO approach typically takes eighteen to twenty-four months to implement, but the transformation is largely complete upon conversion.

Business process outsourcing. BPO is sometimes referred to as the transfer then transform approach. Under this alternative, the vendor takes over the existing workforce administration environment, including the current systems and perhaps even the staff members performing the services. Once the transfer is complete, the vendor may begin to transform processes, procedures, and systems onto some common technologies and preferred approaches throughout the term of the relationship.

Although all of those alternatives are available, the momentum in workforce administration seems to be behind outsourcing the entire workforce administration function through the HRO or BPO strategies.

No reliable market data are available with respect to the use of ASP relationships for workforce administration, but the percentages are probably quite small. Moreover, the existence of an ASP relationship does not necessarily reflect a strategic decision by HR but is more likely to reflect an IT-related decision by the organization as a whole.

The Right Strategy for Your Organization

Workforce administration is the foundation for your organization's flexibility to outsource many other HR functions that are covered later in this book. Therefore, you should make any decision to outsource this function with care and with a clear understanding of its effect on your other outsourcing alternatives.

The first two outsourcing solutions identified above, hiring an application service provider or implementing a point solution, are largely tactical solutions. Neither of those solutions is truly an outsourced solution in its purest sense, because your organization will still retain primary responsibility for the overall delivery of workforce administration services. Therefore, those solutions are typically attractive if your organization is not yet ready to embrace the full-scale outsourcing of workforce administration, yet would like to secure some kind of marginal cost savings or realignment of corporate resources by outsourcing just certain features of workforce administration.

The latter two outsourcing solutions represent a wholesale change in the manner in which your organization provides workforce administration services to your employees. The two approaches will look the most attractive to organizations seeking to "transform" the HR function into a more strategic entity by outsourcing the administrative and transactional components so that the residual HR function can focus more of its time and attention on the needs of the business.

Key Considerations

Several significant factors will affect not only your organization's potential solutions, but also whether your company can reasonably expect to be able to outsource those functions. The factors are described in Table 9.1.

Table 9.1

Workforce Administration: Key Factors

Factor	Considerations
Transformation	Many organizations are interested in transforming the HR function into a model that is based on having shared service centers, centers of excellence, and business partners. Sometimes this restructuring of the HR function can be simplified and facilitated by establishing an outsourcing relationship for the shared service center component.
Cost	Some organizations will be able to provide workforce administration services at a lower cost than outsourced solutions, unless they are willing to entertain allowing the providers to use offshore resources (see below).
Offshoring	Most outsourcing organizations will want to use offshore resources to perform certain aspects of workforce administration. Buyers of those services need to be prepared to discuss their willingness to have aspects of this function performed outside the United States.
Depreciation	Many organizations have made significant investments in their HRIS and related functional HR systems over the past few years. Some of those organizations elected to capitalize those investments and to depreciate those costs over the usable life of the software. Such organizations may not be willing to consider outsourcing alternatives that might require them to accelerate the recognition of these deferred costs.
Technology	Many organizations are finding it difficult to sustain their investments in their HRIS platforms. Outsourcing can be a solution for avoiding the need to compete for capital expenditures with the rest of the business.
Global requirements	Many organizations are in the midst of integrating their global operations onto a single HR database or reporting system. Outsourcing may enable those organizations to accelerate their movement to common systems and procedures.
Global expansion	Some organizations are rapidly deploying their workforce around the world, including into emerging market countries like China or India. Outsourcing may allow those organizations to leverage existing provider locations in such countries rather than creating their own HR functions there.
Scalability	Organizations that are expected to grow (or shrink) rapidly over the next few years may find that outsourcing will allow them to provide the right level of HR support services to match changing needs.

Services to Outsource in Conjunction with Workforce Administration

As indicated above, workforce administration is usually outsourced in conjunction with certain other HR functions. In particular, some functions, such as compensation administration or performance management, cannot really be outsourced on a standalone basis and are generally outsourced only in conjunction with workforce administration. Other functions, such as benefits administration, have historically been outsourced on a standalone basis and, therefore, should not affect your decision making for this service.

Figure 9.1 summarizes the data from more than fifty workforce administration outsourcing relationships to provide a snapshot of which HR functions other organizations have elected to combine with their workforce administration relationship in contrast to those services that either are retained internally or have been outsourced separately. As shown, most organizations have combined payroll and benefits administration with their workforce administration relationship. And many companies have also included other key functional areas, such as compensation and learning.

Figure 9.1
Other HR Functions Outsourced with Workforce Administration

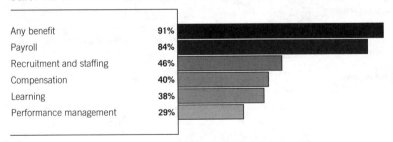

Any benefit	91%
Payroll	84%
Recruitment and staffing	46%
Compensation	40%
Learning	38%
Performance management	29%

Source: Gildner & Associates Prevalance Database™

The Future of Human Resource Information Systems

Today, the major manufacturers of human resource information systems have penetrated more than 90 percent of large organizations. The most common model for workforce administration today is an internal solution using an HRIS that was either developed internally or purchased and installed. However, we have probably already seen the peak of the use of this approach, because the migration to outsourcing of this function has begun in earnest. Figure 9.2 illustrates the relative prevalence of outsourcing workforce administration among large organizations since 1998. As shown, outsourcing's relative share of the industry has grown from less than 1 percent to more than 8 percent in just six years. It appears that workforce administration has begun a similar trajectory toward outsourcing, as have many functions before it, particularly benefits administration. The market for those services is growing at an exponential rate, and we would expect that about 30 percent of large organizations will have adopted an outsourcing solution for workforce administration by 2010.

Figure 9.2

Workforce Administration: The Prevalence of Outsourcing

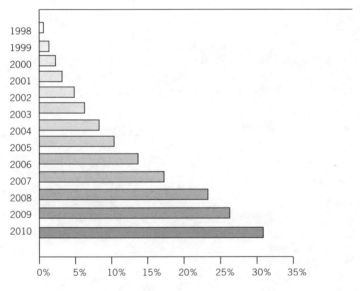

Another indication of the role that outsourcing is taking in the transformation of workforce administration was its role in the takeover of PeopleSoft by Oracle Corporation. In testimony before the Justice Department on the effect of the combination from an antitrust perspective, one of Oracle's defenses was that there were a number of new competitors in the HRIS market in the form of outsourcing organizations. Several of the outsourcing providers in the workforce administration market are developing their own HRIS applications that are designed in a one-to-many architecture that can support multiple clients simultaneously. We would expect at least some of the current purveyors of HRIS applications to form alliances or to merge with an outsourcing partner over the next few years in an attempt to protect their existing market share.

CHAPTER 10
Outsourcing Benefits Administration

Benefits administration, particularly administration of 401(k) plans, was the first functional area within human resources to be outsourced on a comprehensive basis. Before the advent of bundled 401(k) plan administration in the 1980s, virtually all employers retained responsibility for all HR administration internally. Up until that time, outsourcing was a tactic used solely for highly specialized functions, such as claims adjudication, qualified domestic relations order (QDRO) administration, or participant recordkeeping aspects of defined contribution plan administration. Often, the vendor for those services was the company's benefits or actuarial consulting firm.

But beginning in the late 1970s, a new model for 401(k) plan administration was invented. That model included not only participant recordkeeping services but also twenty-four hours per day, seven day per week, access through voice response technology, which was supplemented by 800-number call centers. In addition, vendors such as Fidelity and Merrill Lynch offered integrated trust and investment management services to create a one-stop shopping approach to defined contribution plan administration. Better yet, such companies offered to subsidize the cost of plan administration through their investment management fees, thus driving down the cost of administration to plan sponsors by shifting those costs to plan participants. In the course of just a single decade, more than 50 percent of all large plan sponsors outsourced their 401(k) plan administration to one of the bundled providers offering this new solution—and the outsourcing movement in HR was born.

Today, there are a number of providers not only for defined contribution administration but also for defined benefit administration plus health and welfare administration. Benefits administration is the most mature outsourcing marketplace of all the functional areas within HR. It is characterized by short implementation timeframes, state-of-the-art technology, declining prices, and competition that is based on enhancements to the services provided to plan participants and sponsors. Benefits administration provides a window into the potential of outsourcing for other HR functions in the future.

Definition of Benefits Administration

Benefits administration is typically described as the support for the three major benefit programs offered by most large employers:

- Defined benefit plan administration

- Defined contribution plan administration

- Health and welfare plan administration

Benefits administration is also the broad functional category that includes the following set of HR functions and activities:

- Claims adjudication

- Medical, life, disability, dental, vision, or other carrier relationships

- Integrated disability management

- Specialized functions such as COBRA, FSA, or QDRO administration

Certain other HR functions are also often included in benefits administration, but they could alternatively be considered part of compensation administration. Those functions include

- Stock purchase and stock option administration

- Nonqualified defined benefit and defined contribution plan administration

- Executive benefit plan administration

Prevalence of Outsourcing

Benefits administration is the most frequently outsourced function in human resources today. Among large employers, nearly 100 percent outsource their defined contribution plan administration. And the trend among the other benefit programs has been steadily climbing for more than a decade. Figure 10.1 illustrates the relative prevalence of outsourcing among large companies.

Figure 10.1
Benefits Administration: Prevalence of Outsourcing

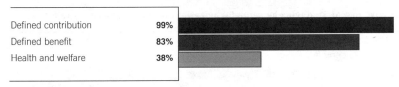

Defined contribution	99%	
Defined benefit	83%	
Health and welfare	38%	

Source: Gildner & Associates Prevalence Database™
for large employers (those with more than 10,000 employees)

Marketplace Alternatives

Four different solutions are available for outsourcing benefits administration. For purposes of this chapter, we will discuss only those solutions that are relatively significant in scope. We would consider any subprocess outsourcing solutions in benefits administration, such as COBRA administration, to be tactical solutions used in conjunction with an internal administration strategy.

The marketplace alternatives available today for adopting an outsourced approach to benefits administration include the following:

Point solutions. These solutions are sometimes called co-sourcing solutions. In this approach, the vendor typically provides the software application solution for the benefits program, sometimes in conjunction with a certain level of call center support. However, the client retains responsibility for the overall success of the delivery function and for any aspects of the administration not performed by the vendor.

Best-in-class. This is the industry name for selecting outsourcing vendors on the basis of the assessment that they provided the best service for each functional area, without regard to a desire to adopt either an integrated retirement or total benefits outsourcing (TBO) strategy as described below.

Integrated retirement. This is the industry terminology for having both defined benefit and defined contribution plans administered by a single organization.

Total benefits outsourcing. TBO is the commonly used term for outsourcing all benefits administration to a single provider.

Figure 10.2 illustrates the relative use of those various outsourcing strategies by large organizations for each of the three major functional areas within benefits administration.

Figure 10.2
Relative Use of Strategies by Large Organizations for Benefits Administration

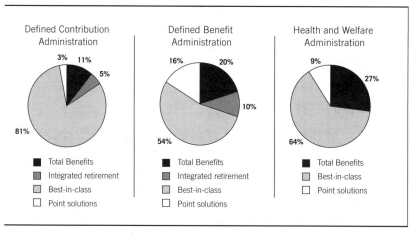

Source: Gildner & Associates Prevalence Database™

The Right Strategy for Your Organization

The advantage of outsourcing benefits administration has become a foregone conclusion in most large organizations today. The vendor service offerings are so mature that it is unlikely that any organization can cost-effectively provide similar functionality to participants. The first outsourcing solution identified above—implementing a point solution—is largely a tactical solution because your organization will still retain primary responsibility for the overall delivery of benefits administration services. Therefore, this solution is typically attractive if your organization is not yet ready to embrace the full-scale outsourcing of benefits administration, yet would like to secure some kind of marginal cost savings or realignment of corporate resources by outsourcing just certain features of benefits administration.

The other outsourcing solutions—best-in-class, integrated retirement, and TBO—represent a wholesale change in the manner in which your organization provides benefits administration services to your employees. They are the approaches that will look the most attractive to organizations that are seeking to transform the benefits function into a more strategic entity by outsourcing the administrative and transactional components so that the residual benefits function can focus more of its time and attention on how to design and communicate those programs to support the needs and objectives of the business.

Key Considerations

Table 10.1 describes several significant factors. Those factors not only will affect your organization's potential solutions but also will determine whether your company can reasonably expect to be able to outsource the functions.

Services to Outsource in Conjunction with Benefits Administration

As indicated in the introduction to this chapter, the benefits administration market has matured on a freestanding basis. It is absolutely possible to outsource benefits administration as a single function without limiting your organization's ability to make other HR outsourcing decisions.

However, there are still some functions that would seem to integrate nicely with benefits administration. One obvious integration candidate would be payroll administration, given that many benefit programs require employee contributions, premium deductions, or some other type of interface between payroll and benefits. Another long-term candidate would be compensation administration, because employee benefits are really just another form of compensation, and we would expect opportunities to communicate the value of total compensation to increase. Finally, executive compensation is often tightly linked with benefit plan administration either in the form of the nonqualified component of the retirement programs or in the form of

Table 10.1

Benefits Administration: Key Factors

Factor	Considerations
Cost	Some organizations are able to provide benefits administration services at a lower cost than an outsourced solution. Therefore, cost may be an inhibiting factor for some organizations that are considering outsourcing this function. However, in recent years, outsourcing costs in the industry have generally been falling.
Offshoring	Some outsourcing organizations have begun to use offshore resources to perform certain aspects of benefits administration. Buyers of those services need to be prepared to discuss their willingness to have aspects of this function performed outside the United States, particularly given concerns about data privacy in health care.
Technology	Outsourcing benefits administration is often driven by a desire to gain access to new and enhanced technology. Service providers generally offer robust automated functionality.
Compliance	Many aspects of benefits administration are both complex and associated with legislated requirements. Key examples of complex areas would include compliance with COBRA, HIPAA, or data privacy issues. The risks associated with noncompliance are large relative to the cost of administration. Service providers in benefits administration are generally considered more likely to perform services in accordance with applicable legislative rules and regulations.
Quality of services	Although there will always be some debate about the quality of outsourced services relative to internally provided services, the provider community is able to guarantee a relatively consistent experience for employee and participant users of the services. The outsourcing model is somewhat less susceptible to turnover of key individuals.
Enhanced services	The competitive nature of the benefits administration marketplace has led many providers to offer enhancements to their services far beyond mere administration capabilities. It is possible to gain access to many value-added services through outsourcing with little or no incremental investment.

other deferred compensation arrangements that are designed to mimic defined contribution plans. So, again from a communications vantage point, the integration of benefits and compensation administration would seem to have its advantages.

The Future of Outsourced Benefits Administration

The benefits outsourcing marketplace is very mature, and the competition among the providers has been effective at driving down operating costs year after year. Better yet, the providers are actively solving difficult aspects of benefits administration that have been intractable problems for individual employers. A perfect example is the time lag between hire and establishment of benefit eligibility or between termination and expiration of benefit eligibility. The vendor community is currently in the midst of integrating their eligibility systems with those of many of the major health and welfare carriers to entirely eliminate those time lags. This kind of innovation has been made possible only by the advent of the outsourcing industry and the market-competitive forces it has created among the vendors.

Other examples of innovation in the benefits outsourcing marketplace follow:

- Integrated financial advice services as part of 401(k) plan administration

- Medical plan option modeling as part of the annual enrollment process

- Integrated retirement statements for participants, communicating the value of their participation in both the defined benefit and the defined contribution plans

- Primary care physician identification and selection

- Debit card purchases in conjunction with FSA accounts

Those and similar enhancements have been emerging over the past decade, and they can typically be adopted at little or no cost to plan sponsors. We expect continuing innovation in the benefits administration marketplace as the providers strive to distinguish their services from those offered by their competitors.

CHAPTER 11
Outsourcing Payroll Administration

There is more confusion about outsourcing payroll administration than about outsourcing any other function within human resources. More specifically, there is an almost universal belief that everyone outsources payroll administration. In reality, that belief is a myth—at least among large employers.

Another factor that often complicates a discussion of outsourcing payroll administration is the fact that the payroll function often reports to the finance department, rather than the HR department. Many organizations have aligned payroll with finance internally because of their concerns about maintaining effective financial controls over such a large cost of doing business. However, from an employee-servicing perspective, there are clear and compelling synergies for the integration not only of workforce administration and payroll, but also of benefits and compensation administration.

The final factor that increases confusion in this area is the definition of payroll administration itself. The model for payroll administration among small organizations is generally limited to the production of paychecks and the reporting of withholdings to taxing entities. But as we will describe in this chapter, payroll administration includes much more than check processing.

Definition of Payroll Administration

Payroll administration generally consists of the following functions and services:

- Employee data capture and maintenance for items that affect payroll

- Gross-to-net processing

- Paycheck and advice production and distribution

- Tax withholding and reporting

It also includes some of the more complex administrative processes, such as

- Garnishment and lien administration

- Cash management and payroll accounting

In addition, some other complex functions may be integrated with payroll administration, such as

- Time and attendance data capture and reporting

- Labor management reporting and scheduling

Prevalence of Payroll Outsourcing

As indicated in the introduction to this chapter, payroll administration is frequently outsourced by smaller organizations but is infrequently outsourced by large organizations. The American Payroll Association has published a particularly comprehensive study on the prevalence of outsourcing in payroll administration. The results of that study are presented in Figure 11.1. As shown in the figure, although the majority of small companies outsource payroll, the percentage that use the services of a third-party vendor drops dramatically as the size of the underlying organization increases.

The trend toward outsourcing payroll administration has been accelerating over the past five years among larger companies. However, the adoption of outsourcing of payroll administration may grow at a somewhat slower rate than workforce administration because payroll is often a finance function and, therefore, sometimes not included in scope along with other HR functions.

Figure 11.1
Payroll Outsourcing by Company Size

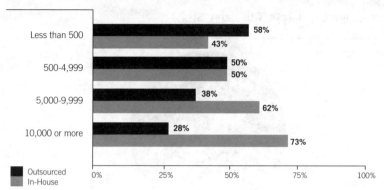

Total percentages exceed 100% due to rounding. Source: Goldman, Sachs & Co. and American Payroll Association

Marketplace Alternatives

Three major solutions are available for outsourcing payroll administration. For purposes of this chapter, we will discuss only those solutions that are relatively significant in scope. We would consider any subprocess outsourcing solutions in payroll administration, such as check printing and distribution, to be tactical solutions used in conjunction with an internal administration strategy.

The alternatives available for adopting an outsourced approach to payroll administration include the following:

Point solutions. In this approach, the vendor typically performs the gross-to-net processing and tax reporting for payroll administration, perhaps with some call center support. Nevertheless, the client is still responsible for the overall success of the delivery function and for any aspects of the administration that the vendor does not perform.

Single Process Outsourcing. This is the industry terminology for selecting one vendor to perform end-to-end payroll administration processing on a standalone basis.

Integrated HR and Payroll Outsourcing. This is the commonly used term for outsourcing payroll administration in conjunction with a larger outsourcing arrangement that includes workforce administration. In this kind of solution, the HRIS and payroll administration systems are based on an integrated data model and employee-servicing environment.

Figure 11.2
Payroll Administration
Percentange of Employers Utilizing Strategy

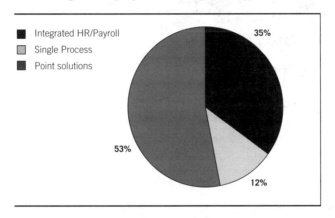

Source: Gildner & Associates Prevalence Database TM for large employers
(those with more than 10,000 employees)

Figure 11.2 illustrates the relative use of the various outsourcing strategies by large organizations.

The Right Strategy for Your Organization

Payroll administration is considered one of the least strategic functions within human resources. That fact would suggest that the relative cost-effectiveness of the solutions available should be given greater weight than might be the case for other HR functions. The point solutions described above are largely tactical solutions. They are not really outsourced solutions in the purest sense, because your organization will still retain primary responsibility for the overall delivery of payroll administration services. Therefore, they will typically be attractive only if they enable your organization to reduce its delivery costs.

Similarly, the single process outsourcing solution described above has its own limitations. It has the advantage of shifting the locus of responsibility for payroll administration from your organization to a third-party provider. However, the primary reason for making such a change is still likely to be a neutral or positive business case for the function.

Later in this chapter, we describe some other HR functions that have a natural synergy with payroll administration. Such synergies can often provide strategic value above and beyond a pure comparison of the cost of delivery. But only an integrated HR–payroll or benefits–payroll solution is likely to capture those synergies.

Key Considerations

Several factors will affect the solutions that your organization is able to adopt. Whether your company can reasonably expect to be able to outsource such functions will depend on the factors shown in Table 11.1.

Table 11.1

Payroll Administration: Key Factors

Factor	Considerations
Cost	Some organizations with high volume payroll operations are able to perform payroll administration on a very cost-effective basis internally. Therefore, cost may be an inhibiting factor for some organizations that might otherwise like to outsource this nonstrategic function.
Volume	The annual volume and pattern of payments is a key driver of payroll administration costs. If an organization needs to produce large volumes of payments in short periods of time, it may need to install excess internal capacity to meet those needs, a step that is often inefficient.
Compliance	Many organizations would like to shift the responsibility for compliance with federal, state, and local tax laws to an external organization that monitors such legislation on behalf of multiple clients.
Systems capabilities	Some organizations use their payroll system as a substitute for an HR management system application. For such companies, outsourcing payroll administration is similar to outsourcing workforce administration.
Technology	Many organizations are reluctant to invest in the new technology required to support payroll administration in a best-practices fashion. Such technologies might include imaging, employee and manager self-service, and high-speed printing and fulfillment capability.
Enhanced services	Some external organizations are able to provide various service offerings that may be perceived as providing added value to payroll administration. Such services include online advice processing, integrated pay and benefits illustrations, or paycheck modeling.

Services to Outsource in Conjunction with Payroll Administration

There are some natural synergies between payroll administration and certain other HR functions. Payroll administration requires a careful integration with basic employment status changes, such as hires, terminations, and leaves; therefore, it is a prime candidate for integration with workforce administration. Payroll administration also is closely aligned with compensation administration, both because it is a source of employee salary data and because it involves the administration of salary and bonus programs. Finally, many benefit plans require employee-paid premiums or allow for voluntary payroll deductions, suggesting that there are advantages to integrating payroll and benefits administration.

In addition, unlike most other HR functions, some other business functions are often linked to payroll administration. As indicated above, those functions include

- Time and attendance data capture and tracking

- Labor management reporting and scheduling.

In addition, payroll administration has often been associated with the following finance functions:

- Expense reimbursement

- Accounts payable administration

Not all HR vendors perform those functions. Therefore, if your organization currently supports some of the associated functions in an internal shared services department, you cannot presume that they can be outsourced along with the payroll function itself. It may be necessary either to retain the processes or to find an alternate solution for those services not offered by the outsourcing vendor.

The Future of Outsourced Payroll Administration

The demand for outsourced payroll administration is almost certain to accelerate among larger organizations. Historically, cost-effective solutions have not been available for such organizations, but now those solutions are emerging. Although it is a myth that every organization outsources payroll, it is generally accepted that outsourcing payroll make sense, because payroll administration is a purely transactional function. Few organizations believe that performing payroll administration internally has strategic value.

The only uncertainty in the market today is whether companies will seek best-in-class providers for payroll administration or whether they will seek to adopt a solution that is integrated with either workforce administration or benefits administration. We suspect there will be good arguments for either approach and that the marketplace will remain divided with respect to the optimal strategy for payroll administration, much as the benefits administration marketplace is divided among the various solutions available. However, over the coming decades, we would expect a general shift toward the integration of payroll and workforce administration and the transfer of responsibility for payroll administration from the finance department to the HR department.

CHAPTER 12

Outsourcing Recruiting and Staffing

For years, many organizations have used outsourcing for certain components of the recruiting and staffing function. Getting some third-party specialized assistance for executive recruiting or temporary staffing is common. More recently, companies have turned to third-party software to help them with applicant tracking or job postings. Internet sites such as Monster.com and CareerBuilder.com have emerged as the new venue for connecting employers with potential employees.

Although the various subprocess outsourcing strategies are common, only recently have we seen organizations begin to explore outsourcing the entire recruiting and staffing function. In this chapter, we will discuss the emerging options available for this critical HR activity.

Recruiting and staffing administration, sometimes called *talent supply*, consists of the following basic functions and services:

• Job requisition and posting

• Applicant tracking

• Candidate sourcing (both internal and external)

• Preplacement verification and screening

• Offer management

It also includes some of the more complex administrative processes, including

• Executive recruitment and placement

• University relations and campus recruiting

• Internship programs

• Branding programs

In addition, a couple of other HR functions may be integrated with recruiting and staffing administration:

• Global mobility and domestic relocation

• Contingent workforce administration

Prevalence of Outsourcing

As indicated in the introduction to this chapter, although subprocess outsourcing has often been used selectively to support this function, overall responsibility for the recruiting and staffing function has typically remained an internal function. A new trend is emerging toward the outsourcing of this functional area, either on a standalone basis or in conjunction with workforce administration.

Today, fewer than 5 percent of large organizations outsource their recruiting and staffing. However, that percentage has been growing in lockstep with the growth of outsourcing workforce administration.

Marketplace Alternatives

Three different solutions are available for outsourcing recruiting and staffing administration. For purposes of this chapter, we will discuss only outsourcing solutions that are relatively significant in scope. We would consider any subprocess outsourcing solutions in recruiting and staffing administration, such as placing executives or using an external job board, to be tactical solutions exercised in conjunction with an internal administration strategy.

The marketplace alternatives available today for adopting a truly outsourced approach to recruiting and staffing administration include the following:

Point solutions. In this approach, the vendor typically performs all of the support related to internal and external job requisition and posting, sometimes in conjunction with a certain level of call center support. The client, however, retains responsibility for the overall success of the recruiting and staffing function and for any aspects of the administration that the vendor does not perform.

Single process outsourcing. Under this method, a single vendor performs the end-to-end recruiting and staffing function on a stand-alone basis.

Integrated HR outsourcing. In this approach, a company elects to outsource its recruiting and staffing administration in conjunction with a larger outsourcing arrangement that includes workforce administration.

The vast majority of outsourced recruiting and staffing relationships are established in conjunction with outsourcing workforce administration. Only a handful of organizations have outsourced this function as a separate standalone relationship, and a similar small number of organizations have established a point solution type of relationship.

The Right Strategy for Your Organization

Recruiting and staffing administration is considered to be one of the more strategic functions within human resources. In particular, many organizations work hard to gain a competitive advantage that is based on their hiring practices. Therefore, this function deserves a certain amount of extra scrutiny when an organization is considering it as a candidate for outsourcing. For example, it would not be unusual for a high-technology firm to want to retain responsibility for its branding program, its university relations, and perhaps its recruitment of software engineers.

In other situations, the aspect of recruiting and staffing that is strategic is the importance of filling the positions themselves. For example, a retail organization with 80 to 100 percent turnover each year must be outstanding at filling open positions with acceptably qualified candidates on a continuous basis.

Despite those nuances, much of recruiting and staffing administration is purely transactional in nature and is not strategic to any organization. All organizations must post open positions, collect applicants, and identify candidates. All organizations must prescreen applicants, extend job offers, move employees between cities, and communicate the hiring decision internally to ensure that security, facilities, and other internal functions are ready to accept the new employee. And even in the most esoteric research or engineering businesses, a large proportion of the staff is likely to be administrative or managerial in nature and may not require special treatment in the recruitment process. All of those functions are good candidates for outsourcing even within firms with specialized needs.

Table 12.1

Recruiting and Staffing Administration: Key Factors

Factor	Considerations
Recruiting model	Is the recruiting function performed by a dedicated recruiting staff member, or are most positions filled by managers performing their own recruiting? If the latter, it may be difficult to establish a business case for using an external provider because the cost of recruiting is obscured in operating costs.
Volume	How many open positions will need to be filled within your organization each year? If the volume is low, then your organization may be able to leverage additional capabilities for identifying candidates by leveraging an external provider's greater scale of operations. If the volume is high, then you may be more interested in the provider's ability to increase productivity and to decrease the time required to fill open positions.
Scalability	Do the needs of your organization for candidates either fluctuate seasonally within a given year or vary from year to year? If your demand is uneven or sporadic, there may be an opportunity to convert high fixed costs into variable expenses by structuring a relationship that is based on the number of positions filled.
Geographic locations	Do the needs of your organization for candidates vary among geographically dispersed locations? Large external providers may offer a greater distribution of their recruiting network, thus enabling them to have a local market presence in more job markets.
Specialized functions	Does your organization attempt to differentiate itself through the hiring of certain critical specialized functions? If so, those positions may be ones that should be considered for retaining internally.
Technology	Would your organization benefit from new technology, such as applicant tracking systems, to support the function? Establishing a relationship with an external provider may be a more cost-effective manner of gaining access to new technologies than purchasing and installing them within your own organization.

Key Considerations

Factors that will affect not only your organization's potential solutions, but also whether or not your company can reasonably expect to be able to outsource these functions are described in Table 12.1.

Services to Outsource in Conjunction with Recruiting and Staffing Administration

Most organizations that outsource recruiting and staffing do so in conjunction with workforce administration. All of the data required to track applicants, to establish new hire records, to identify open positions, and to monitor turnover is usually either maintained in or integrated with the employee data being supported under workforce administration. As a result, natural synergies are created by outsourcing those services on an integrated basis.

Two or three other significant functions are often outsourced in conjunction with recruiting and staffing administration. The first one is contingent workforce administration. External providers are usually willing to manage the tracking and administration related to the use of temporary staffing by the organization. But they may also be able to add value by reducing the cost of acquiring such temporary labor. It is not uncommon for large organizations to have dozens, if not hundreds, of local temporary staffing relationships. The outsourcing vendors are rationalizing the acquisition of those employees into a handful of regional or national relationships. This approach simplifies administration while simultaneously leveraging buying power across the vendors' multiple clients.

The other functions that are often outsourced in conjunction with recruiting and staffing are domestic relocation and global mobility. Obviously, helping job candidates get transferred to the appropriate location is an integral part of filling certain openings. The process of outsourcing those subprocesses is described in Chapter 15.

The Future of Outsourced Recruiting and Staffing Administration

The marketplace for recruiting and staffing administration has high potential. Recruiting and staffing administration is a functional area that is classically well suited for outsourcing from several perspectives. First, it is a function that can be technologically enabled. To manage the sheer volume of resumes and job applicants, a company must have automated systems for capturing and tracking the information. Once the data have been captured electronically, technology can be used to match job requirements with applicants' skills to help identify better candidates—all without human intervention.

There is also growing evidence that the productivity of outsourcing vendors may be much higher than that of their internal counterparts. Outsourcing organizations have several advantages relative to an internal recruiting function as follows:

- The outsourcing vendors have national networks of recruiters located in all major job markets.

- The recruiters have a consistent pipeline of jobs to be filled, allowing them to remain "in the market" at all times.

- Clients with smaller or infrequent demand for new candidates can leverage the capabilities of the providers in more local labor markets.

- Because they represent multiple clients, outsourcing organizations are more scalable than internal functions and can react more easily to the changing needs of any individual business for more or fewer new hires.

- The recruiters are supported by more advanced and integrated technology than most individual organizations have been willing to provide.

The result of those advantages is that we are beginning to see dramatic increases in productivity. Where the typical internal recruiter places 100 to150 applicants into positions in a given year, external vendors are achieving rates as high as 300 to 400 applicants placed annually. Given this productivity advantage, we would expect many employers to turn to outsourcing as a more cost-effective solution for at least their nonstrategic hiring needs.

CHAPTER 13
Outsourcing Compensation Administration

Compensation administration is among the more specialized functions in most organizations. Like other specialized areas, the function has historically used third-party services and systems to support the most complex aspects of compensation administration. For example, many organizations use the services of an external provider to supply job evaluation systems, salary surveys, or executive compensation design consulting. But compensation administration itself has almost always been delivered internally in large organizations. Today, that's beginning to change, and outsourcing solutions are starting to emerge.

Compensation administration consists of the following basic functions and services:

- Job evaluation and classification

- Salary and bonus administration

- Overtime, commission, and other special payment administration

- Stock option, stock purchase, and other deferred compensation arrangements

- Paid time-off administration

- Employee recognition programs

It also includes some of the more complex administrative processes, such as

- Executive compensation and benefits administration

- Salary survey analysis

In addition, a couple of other HR functions may be integrated with compensation administration:

- Expatriate administration

- Severance administration

Prevalence of Outsourcing

As indicated in the introduction to this chapter, though subprocess outsourcing has often been used selectively to support this function, overall responsibility for the compensation administration function has typically remained an internal function. However, some companies have started to outsource compensation administration in conjunction with workforce administration. But point solutions or standalone single process solutions for outsourcing are very uncommon at this time. Today, fewer than 5 percent of large organizations outsource compensation administration.

Marketplace Alternatives

Solutions available for outsourcing compensation administration are fairly limited. In particular, few, if any, companies have adopted either a point solution or single process outsourcing approach for compensation administration. Instead, most organizations still perform compensation administration internally, perhaps using external firms for a few specific functions.

In this chapter, we discuss outsourcing solutions that are relatively significant in scope. We would consider any subprocess outsourcing solutions in compensation administration, such as participating in salary surveys or hiring a stock purchase administration provider, to be tactical solutions used in conjunction with an internal administration strategy.

The marketplace alternatives available today for adopting a truly outsourced approach to compensation administration include the following:

Point solutions. In this approach, the vendor typically provides a hosted software solution to support the compensation administration process. Sometimes the vendor also provides a certain level of call center support. However, the client retains responsibility for the overall success of the compensation administration function and for any aspects of the administration not performed by the vendor. Point solutions for compensation administration are very limited in scope at this time and are usually associated with the adoption of an external portal for employee self-service.

Single process outsourcing. Under single process outsourcing, the organization would select one vendor to perform its end-to-end compensation administration on a standalone basis. We are not aware of any organizations that use this approach to compensation administration.

Integrated HR outsourcing. This approach for outsourcing compensation administration is the one most commonly used at present. In particular, compensation administration is outsourced in conjunction with a larger outsourcing arrangement that includes workforce administration.

The Right Strategy for Your Organization

There are few decisions to make with respect to outsourcing compensation administration. Most companies are going to continue to perform this function internally until either they outsource workforce administration or the marketplace service offerings mature. Organizations with current specific needs in compensation administration should search for more tactical, subprocess outsourcing solutions to supplement or enhance their current services. An example of this approach would be to outsource expatriate administration, which is a subprocess specialty within compensation administration that has an established vendor community and is described in Chapter 15.

But for organizations that are considering outsourcing workforce administration, compensation administration is a natural extension of that relationship. Most of the workforce administration vendors have at least salary and bonus administration capabilities that are linked to their employee and manager self-service environment. With those tools in place, they are well positioned to take over many of the more mundane tasks associated with compensation administration.

Key Considerations

Many factors will affect your organization's potential solutions. Those factors will also determine whether your company can reasonably expect to be able to outsource compensation administration functions. The factors are described in Table 13.1.

Table 13.1
Compensation Administration: Key Factors

Factor	Considerations
Annual merit and bonus programs	The external vendor systems are designed to carefully control and monitor the administration of these programs on a cascading basis up the management chain. This control mechanism may enable some companies to manage salary budgets more effectively.
Executive compensation	Many organizations consider the design and administration of their executive compensation programs to be a particularly high-touch activity. Such activities may not be good candidates for outsourcing, particularly in an immature market.
Stock programs	Stock program administration is complex. These services may be better handled in a separate outsourcing arrangement with a vendor that specializes in such services.
Expatriate administration	Expatriate administration has a relatively mature marketplace of specialty providers. These services may receive more attention by remaining segregated from the rest of compensation administration.
Enhanced services	External providers are seeking ways to add value to compensation administration services. For example, new capabilities are under development that would allow administrators to compare job classifications with salary survey data. In addition, integrated online total compensation statements are available that combine salary, bonus, and employee benefit data to provide a consolidated view of total rewards.

Services to Outsource in Conjunction with Compensation Administration

As indicated above, most organizations that outsource compensation administration have done so in conjunction with workforce administration. But that fact is probably a reflection of the current immaturity of the outsourcing marketplace for compensation and HR administration, and it may change over time.

Several other HR functions seem to fit naturally with an outsourced compensation administration function. The first is payroll administration, which is the ultimate reflection of the salary, bonus, and other payment programs to employees. Although payroll administration has historically been viewed as primarily a finance-type function, we believe that, as the outsourcing marketplace matures, synergies between payroll and compensation administration will emerge. Another functional area that seems to complement compensation administration is benefits administration. After all, employee benefits are merely another type of compensation. Many firms like to communicate the overall value of their total compensation programs, including both salary and benefits. But in the market today, benefits administration is the most mature outsourcing segment, and compensation administration is among the least mature. Over time, we would expect those services either to merge or at least to develop a strong integration in their presentation and communication to employees. The common industry term for the combination of compensation and benefits administration is *rewards administration*.

Finally, it might make sense to consider outsourcing talent development, including performance management, with compensation administration, particularly if the organization is interested in establishing more direct links between performance and compensation. Increases in compensation can often provide the incentive for employees to participate more actively in learning and other professional development activities. Establishing and communicating more integration between compensation and professional development would seem to be natural.

The Future of Outsourced Compensation Administration

Compensation administration is another HR function that appears to be poised to benefit significantly from outsourcing. Historically, the compensation function has not been an area where organizations have invested heavily in technology or enhanced capabilities. Yet it is a function that lends itself perfectly to integrated desktop tools among the administration function, employees, and managers. Although the business case for making investments in those tools has been hard to identify in individual organizations, the vendor community has a completely different dynamic at work—market competition.

Compensation administration has been one of the areas that has attracted the immediate attention of the outsourcing community as a way to differentiate a vendor's services not only from internal alternatives but also from the services of competitors. Some vendors already have compensation consulting practices that can provide survey data or other job evaluation tools that can be integrated into the outsourcing service offering. The attractiveness of outsourcing compensation administration can be expected to evolve rapidly as the vendors rush to expand their service offerings.

CHAPTER 14
Outsourcing Talent Development Administration

Talent development is a new term in the vocabulary of HR administration. It includes all of the areas within HR that have traditionally been focused on the identification and development of individual employees. Thus, it includes all aspects of learning services and administration, performance management, professional development, organizational development, affirmative action, equal opportunity programs, and succession planning.

As the term talent development suggests, many firms consider their ability to develop talent within their organizations to be a strategic function from which they hope to derive a competitive advantage. Talent development is an area that attracts varying levels of internal investment, depending on the relative value of human capital in the organization's overall strategy. The needs of different organizations can vary dramatically. In fact, the needs within the same organization generally vary. Many companies have allowed each division to create its own learning group, and, until recently, those divisions rarely shared budgets or ideas. Most companies have allocated very little of their internal capital investment toward implementing performance management systems.

Not surprisingly, as a result, common external solutions to support those functions have been slow to emerge in some areas. However, relatively sophisticated service offerings have developed in the area of learning services, including content development, training delivery, and learning management systems. As we will learn in this chapter, an outsourcing market for learning administration is clearly emerging, with signs that the remainder of talent development is not far behind.

Definition of Talent Development

Talent development consists of the following basic functions and services:

- Learning administration, including
  - Course catalog maintenance
  - Content design and development
  - Course registration
  - Content delivery (both electronic and instructor led)
  - Third-party contract management (of content delivery providers, instructors, e-learning vendors, facilities, etc.)
  - Facilities scheduling and management
  - Tracking against employee development plans

- Performance management

- Skills inventorying and management

It also includes some of the more complex administrative processes, such as

- Executive identification and development

- Succession planning

In addition, certain other HR functions are often integrated with talent development, including

- Equal employment opportunity programs

- Affirmative action programs

Prevalence of Outsourcing

As indicated in the introduction to this chapter, although subprocess outsourcing has often been used selectively to support some aspects of learning administration, overall responsibility for the talent development function has typically remained an internal activity. However, some companies have started to outsource broader talent development activities in conjunction with workforce administration. Other companies have established point solutions or standalone single process outsourcing solutions for learning administration, but those solutions are usually limited specifically to learning activities. Talent development remains one of the least outsourced functions today within human resources. Fewer than 5 percent of large organizations outsource the entire integrated talent development process.

Marketplace Alternatives

Many subprocess solutions are available for various aspects of talent development administration. In particular, some companies that have adopted a point solution or subprocess outsourcing approach for various aspects of learning administration. Many more organizations have installed software recordkeeping applications, called *learning management systems* (LMSs), to provide an online course catalog, to launch e-learning content, to register employees for courses, and to track employees' progress against individual training and development goals.

For purposes of this chapter, we will discuss only outsourcing solutions that are relatively significant in scope. We would consider any subprocess outsourcing solutions in talent development administration, such as content development for a particular training course, to be a tactical solution that is used in conjunction with an internal adminis-tration strategy.

The marketplace alternatives available for adopting a truly outsourced approach to talent development administration include the following:

Point solutions. In this approach, the vendor typically provides a hosted LMS to support the learning administration process, many times in conjunction with some call center support. However, the overall success of the talent development function remains with the client, as well as any aspects of the administration that are not performed by the vendor.

Single process outsourcing. Under this alternative, an organization selects one vendor to perform its end-to-end talent development function on a standalone basis. This strategy is seldom used for all of talent development. However, there are several well-established outsourcing relationships for learning administration.

Integrated HR outsourcing. This approach is one that is most commonly used for outsourcing talent development. In it, talent development is outsourced in conjunction with a larger HR outsourcing arrangement that includes workforce administration.

The Right Strategy for Your Organization

The decision with respect to outsourcing talent development depends largely on the issue of timing. If your organization has immediate challenges and needs related to the delivery of learning administration solutions, it is reasonable to evaluate the point solutions and single process outsourcing solutions already available in the market today.

However, if your organization is, at present, able to support its talent development needs internally, then waiting may be the more effective strategy. Alternatively, your organization may want to give more consideration to internal systems development and to the adoption of point solutions in this functional area. As we will discuss in more detail later in this chapter, we believe that the outsourcing industry has embarked on a period of investment in talent development that will produce new tools and services that are not available today. Adopting a delivery strategy that includes maintaining the internal status quo for the next few years is likely to produce significant dividends in the medium term. Note that this strategy also suggests that your organization may want to consider limiting internal investments in this space so that you can more fully leverage the work being performed by the vendor community when, in fact, you are ready to adopt an outsourced solution for this function.

Key Considerations

Several significant factors will affect the potential solutions for your organization (see table 14.1). Those factors will also determine whether your company can reasonably expect to be able to outsource the talent development function.

Table 14.1

Talent Development Administration: Key Factors

Factor	Considerations
Technology	If an organization is considering the purchase and installation of an LMS or a learning content management system or is considering hosting online content, it may find implementing an outsourced solution more cost-effective.
Course registration	Managing the process of registering and removing employees for classes and related activities, such as responding to inquiries, is a nonstrategic activity that lends itself to being supported from a shared services center, either externally or internally.
Learning delivery	Many organizations could benefit from more effective use of online learning techniques, which can be much more cost-effective than classroom delivery. External providers may have more experience and may offer capabilities not available without significant internal investment.
Content design	Much of today's paper-based content is rapidly being converted to e-learning formats, which allow for more efficient delivery. External providers may have established relationships with content designers and more experience with such conversions than internal employees.
Third-party contract management	Many organizations allow their divisions or locations to control their third-party spending on content delivery (i.e., training). It may be possible to capture relatively significant savings by centralizing this contract management with an outsourced provider that has national or multiclient contracts in place for similar services.
Integration	Ideally, learning activities would be closely linked to performance development plans for individual employees. External providers are building integrated talent development platforms that combine learning activities with performance management and compensation administration.

Services to Outsource in Conjunction with Talent Development

The most obvious service to outsource in conjunction with talent development would be compensation administration. There is a natural cycle of events among setting performance goals, thereby making progress against those goals in conjunction with improving skills through learning, year-end performance appraisals, and merit increases and annual bonus determination. While the integration of those functions is evolving, there is a lot of activity within the provider universe directed toward developing the integrated solutions.

The other functions that can be considered for outsourcing in conjunction with talent development have already been identified above. For example, programs such as equal opportunity, diversity, or affirmative action programs are good candidates for inclusion with the outsourcing engagement to ensure that those processes remain associated with the overall talent development strategy and do not drift apart into separate initiatives.

The Future of Outsourced Talent Development Administration

The outsourcing market for the learning administration component within talent development is already maturing. We would expect many companies to avail themselves of external alternatives for either the support of that function through a point solution or the outsourcing of that entire set of activities in the near term on a single-process basis. Over the longer term, we would expect to see the point solutions and single process outsourcing relationships get subsumed into broader talent development relationships that are associated with workforce administration. The rationale for such a consolidation of activities over time is that the natural integration between learning administration, performance development, and succession planning is the ultimate state sought by most large employers. As the outsourcing marketplace begins to offer those integrated solutions, such approaches are likely to be much more attractive than a standalone learning solution.

We would also predict that the area of talent development support will become one of the most competitive aspects of the outsourcing marketplace in the future. There is a significant level of interest among large employers for the tools and processes that might enable them to gain a strategic advantage in developing their internal human capital. Yet today, few solutions in the marketplace address this need. The provider community has already recognized this gap and has seized upon it as a potential area of differentiation of each provider's capabilities from its competitors. Just as benefits administration providers now work to distinguish their modeling and advisory capabilities, we believe broader HR outsourcing providers will seek to distinguish their talent development capabilities. The next few years are likely to produce an intense period of innovation in the talent development arena.

CHAPTER 15

Outsourcing Subprocesses

This book is oriented primarily toward organizations making strategic decisions to outsource one or more HR functions, such as benefits, payroll, or workforce administration. However, many organizations are still using outsourcing as a tactic to solve more specific needs, such as gaining access to experienced resources or minimizing compliance risks. Increasingly, this use of outsourcing for specific tasks within one of the major HR functions is called *subprocess outsourcing*.

In this chapter, we will attempt to identify specific subprocess outsourcing functions that have relatively well-defined outsourcing solutions. This chapter will be useful for organizations that may not yet be ready to adopt outsourcing as their overall human resources delivery strategy, yet are still searching for opportunities to use outsourcing to achieve tactical objectives.

There are good reasons to use outsourcing for certain subprocesses within human resources, even if your organization still subscribes to an internally administered philosophy for HR services. In particular, outsourcing these smaller functions can be attractive for one of two reasons:

1. The function is inherently complex or carries with it legal compliance risks that are disproportionate to the volume of activity (as does, for example, COBRA administration).

2. The function can be provided on a very cost-effective basis by leveraging relatively low volumes within your organization in combination with the much greater scale of activity performed by the vendor across all of its clients.

Readers should note that there are outsourcing alternatives for virtually every aspect of human resources. However, we will focus on some of the specific alternatives that are available today to large organizations that exhibit the following two characteristics:

- They encompass relatively large and complex subprocess functions.

- They have an established outsourcing market for the function.

Candidates for Outsourcing

Using the two characteristics identified above, we would identify the following subprocesses as good candidates for outsourcing:

- Domestic relocation or global mobility

- Expatriate administration

- COBRA administration

- Flexible spending account claims administration

- Pension payroll administration

Each of those processes will be described in somewhat greater detail later in the chapter. Many other candidates for subprocess outsourcing are not covered in detail in this chapter. Processes that may deserve consideration by your organization include the following:

- Applicant tracking

- Employee assistance program administration

- Employment verification services

- Employee background and drug testing

- HIPAA administration

- Integrated disability management

- Payroll tax reporting

- QDRO administration

Any of those processes can be considered for outsourcing by following the processes and procedures outlined throughout this book.

Strategic Considerations

When outsourcing one or more of the functions identified above, an organization should address the issue of what effect, if any, establishing a subprocess outsourcing relationship might have on its ability to establish a more comprehensive outsourcing relationship in the future. In particular, the existence of a large number of subprocess outsourcing relationships can act as an impediment to establishing a more strategic relationship if the services that have already been outsourced overlap with the services provided by the integrated workforce administration provider.

There is no generally accepted best-practice answer to this issue. The real answer depends on a number of factors, including the specific service under consideration and the likely timeframe before a more strategic sourcing decision might be made. We will attempt to provide some context for addressing this issue in each section below. But in the absence of an overarching strategy, it may still make sense to align the termination or expiration provisions of some relationships in anticipation of the emergence of a more integrated strategy.

Domestic Relocation or Global Mobility

Domestic relocation consists of the following basic functions and services:

- Policy and procedure counseling

- Coordination of premove visits and travel

- Current home disposition services

- Destination services, such as school and neighborhood overviews

- Household goods shipping services

- New home acquisition services

- Tax equalization and expense reimbursements services

Global mobility would include not only all of the domestic relocation functions identified above, but also the following supplemental activities:

- Language or cultural orientation training

- Tax counseling

- Vehicle sale and purchase programs

- Coordination of work permits, visas, and local health and safety management

Domestic relocation and global mobility services are perfect candidates for outsourcing because they are obviously specialized services and add no strategic value to the operation of an organization. Typically, organizations outsourcing this kind of a commodity process will increase the importance of price in their selection of a provider.

There is little synergy between supporting domestic or global moves by employees between locations and the remainder of HR administration. Most organizations can make the decision to outsource those services without inhibiting their ability to establish a more strategic outsourcing relationship with a provider of workforce administration, for example. However, there are workforce administration providers that do offer such services or that can provide them in a subcontracted arrangement at potentially lower cost because of increased economies of scale.

Expatriate Administration

Because of its complexity, expatriate administration is being outsourced by an increasing number of organizations. Most organizations use the external services of another organization to advise them of the tax consequences related to the compensation of expatriates. Recently, certain organizations that have been performing either global mobility services or expatriate tax counseling services have begun to offer a more comprehensive set of services centered around supporting those employees. Such services include the following:

- Expatriate policy and procedure counseling

- New assignment briefings

- Ongoing expatriate support

- Localization and transition services

- Repatriation support

For multinational companies that are increasing their movement of key executives around the world, identifying a strategic partner to support their expatriate administration needs would seem to make a lot of sense. Having such a partner would increase the scalability of the function, while also leveraging the provider's experience in new countries, where the client may be interested in expanding. The organizations most likely to be able to effectively outsource this complex function are those that manage expatriates centrally using a common and well-documented set of policies and procedures that can be performed, with few exceptions, by an external provider.

Organizations with current needs in this area should proceed with outsourcing this function without regard to their long-term outsourcing strategy decisions. Although some of the integrated HR outsourcing providers do offer support in this area, its specialization suggests that it will survive as a standalone subprocess function for quite some time. Furthermore, the existing specialty providers have much more experience at this time than the integrated HR outsourcing providers.

COBRA Administration

COBRA administration is one of the most mature market segments in outsourcing. This maturity is attributable to the combination of administrative complexity and the significant level of compliance risk associated with the function. The vast majority of employers, both large and small, outsource COBRA administration at this time.

COBRA administration consists of the following activities:

- Eligibility determination

- Eligible participant notification

- Election capture

- Enrollment processing

- Carrier eligibility reporting

- Premium billing and collections

In some cases, the buyer of COBRA services will retain the responsibility for eligibility determination and participant notification in order to reduce the potential for delays in the notification process.

COBRA administration is clearly a subprocess within the health and welfare benefits administration function. There is quite a bit of integration between normal health and welfare administration and the life events that initiate COBRA. Therefore, most organizations will ultimately want to subsume this activity within any broader health and welfare administration outsourcing relationship that they establish. However, in the near term, buyers should be aware that not all health and welfare administration providers have robust COBRA administration capabilities. Organizations seeking to outsource health and welfare administration should not assume that their provider has much experience with COBRA administration. Instead, some due diligence effort is warranted in this area.

Flexible Spending Account Administration

Most large employers maintain one or more flexible spending accounts in conjunction with their health and welfare benefits program. The most common type of FSA is health care accounts, but dependent care accounts are also offered at many organizations.

- FSA administration includes the following activities:

- Eligibility determination

- Election capture

- Notification of payroll provider of amounts to be withheld

- Employee account maintenance and recordkeeping

- Claim reimbursement processing

More recent enhancements to FSA administration include

- Real-time Internet access to account balance information

- Debit card access to FSAs to avoid the expense reimbursement process

Several types of providers offer FSA administration services, such as

- Specialty providers that offer FSA administration on a standalone basis or in combination with COBRA and HIPAA administration

- Payroll or benefits administration providers that offer the service on either a standalone basis or in conjunction with other primary services

Buyers should recognize that although FSA administration is a relatively mature segment of the outsourcing market, the function is not yet a commodity service. In particular, many of the large HR outsourcing vendors are just starting to offer FSA administration services and may not be as effective as the specialty providers that have years of experience in this area. Therefore, as in the case of COBRA administration, employers that desire to combine those services with a more comprehensive health and welfare administration relationship should perform some due diligence with respect to the provider's experience and capabilities in this area.

Pension Payroll Administration

Pension payroll administration is another subprocess within benefits administration that most companies have historically outsourced. Pension payroll administration consists of the following activities:

- Periodic payment distribution

- Ad hoc payment distribution, such as lump sums, termination cashouts, and temporary supplements

- Federal, state, and local tax withholding and reporting

- Form 1099R production and distribution

- Trust reconciliation and reporting

In some cases, the provider is also responsible for maintaining the data for all payment recipients, including former employees, their spouses, and their dependents. Sometimes, the complexity of the relationship is increased by asking the provider to support some of the following additional activities:

- Nonqualified payment distributions

- Other postemployment program distributions, such as retiree life insurance, survivor benefit, or medical disability payments

- Retiree medical premium withholding and reporting

Historically, the provider for those services has been the organization that was also managing the trust accounts for the defined benefit program. Today, providers increasingly integrate this function with the rest of defined benefit administration in order to provide a seamless experience for participants as they move from employment into retirement. Therefore, organizations should consider consolidating any existing pension payroll provider relationships within defined benefit administration at the time they outsource that function.

The Future of Subprocess Outsourcing

Subprocess outsourcing, as described in this chapter, is likely to maintain its place in human resources as a common tactical solution within many HR functions for some time. However, as the transformation of the HR function transpires over the next decade, most of the subprocess relationships will be subsumed into larger outsourcing engagements involving other transactional components of human resources.

We have already seen a considerable amount of consolidation in these industries. We would expect this industry consolidation to continue within the large client market and to see the specialty providers increasingly move to support the middle and small employer markets where the comprehensive outsourcing approaches are not yet available.

PART IV

Managing Human Resources Outsourcing

CHAPTER 16
Managing the Outsourcing Relationship

Defining Success

One of the enduring challenges in managing outsourcing relationships is the establishment of a commonly accepted definition of success for the relationship. From management's perspective, an outsourcing relationship might be deemed successful if it yielded lower costs of delivery or if it facilitated access to new technologies without capital investment. From an HR generalist or a line manager's perspective, that same relationship might be deemed successful only to the extent it did not create additional—or even just different—work because of a change in the delivery model. And from an employee's perspective, the relationship will be deemed successful depending entirely on each individual's interactions with the provider. When viewed from those varying perspectives, it becomes obvious that success will be in the eye of the beholder. Hence, it is not surprising that defining success is a challenging process.

Another obstacle to reaching consensus on a definition of success is the widely held belief that outsourcing providers should be perfect. Many clients hold to the belief that, because they are paying an external provider for services, perfection is the only acceptable standard of care. This overly simplistic definition of success is destined for failure when applied to any outsourcing relationship, just as it would be if applied to any internal service delivery function. First, there absolutely will be mistakes made in any endeavor performed by human beings. Second, this definition leads to organizational behaviors, such as hiding problems or covering up errors, that can be further detrimental to overall service quality.

The most commonly accepted best practice for defining success is to develop a set of performance criteria that both the client and vendor can consistently measure and monitor. For each criterion, a specific threshold of acceptable performance is defined. Performance at or above that threshold is deemed acceptable—and, hence, successful. Performance below that threshold is deemed unacceptable, and the provider will be expected to implement some kind of remediation plan to improve its performance. This conceptual framework is illustrated in Table 16.1 as it might apply toward the speed of an answer in a call center.

Table 16.1
Performance Management Framework for a Call Center

Level of Performance	Comments	Example
Premium performance	Vendor's performance exceeds expectations. In cases in which exceeding the performance metric generates true value to the client, paying performance premiums might be appropriate.	More than 90% of calls are answered within 30 seconds.
Performance expectation	Vendor meets the expected level of performance as described in the statement of work.	At least 90% of calls are answered within 30 seconds.
Acceptable performance	This level is known as the zone of indifference. Vendor may not be meeting expectations, but service degradation is not serious enough to warrant a financial penalty.	Between 80% and 90% of calls are answered within 30 seconds.
Performance standard	Vendor meets the minimum acceptable level of performance as described in the service level agreement.	At least 80% of calls are answered within 30 seconds.
Unacceptable performance	Vendor is providing poor performance. The value of the service is diminished; therefore, it is appropriate for financial penalties to apply. At this point, the vendor generally should provide client with a remediation plan for correcting the problem.	Fewer than 80% of calls are answered within 30 seconds.

Note that this framework differentiates between performance expectations and performance standards—sometimes referred to as service levels or key performance indicators (KPIs). There is a strong rationale for this bifurcated definition of performance in the documentation of an outsourcing relationship.

There is generally a difference between the agreed-upon performance objectives, or expectations, and the level of performance at which the vendor is willing to put its fees at risk. For example, a vendor may agree that new hire kits will be mailed to new employees within three days of notification by the hiring manager and that this level of service is an appropriate performance expectation. However, that same vendor may not agree to put fees at risk if 100 percent of new hire kits are not mailed within that timeframe. Instead, the appropriate performance standard might be that 90 percent of new hire kits be mailed within three days and that 100 percent be mailed within seven days. The advantage of having a performance expectation is that it sets a clear and unambiguous performance objective so that any kit that is delayed beyond three days is late, even if it will not cause the vendor to incur a financial penalty.

Avoiding Common Mistakes

The most common mistake that the manager of a vendor relationship can make is to rely on hearsay in evaluating the quality of service being provided by the vendor. Unfortunately, without exercising a considerable amount of discipline, many novice vendor managers and even a number of experienced ones will fall into this trap. As a practical matter, part of the vendor manager's role is to assist the provider in resolving problems. Therefore, virtually every problem and issue that arises will be brought to the vendor manager's attention. Over time, it is simple human nature that the vendor management team will begin to have the sense that there are nothing but problems, when, in fact, the vendor may be meeting or exceeding all of its service objectives if measured in a more objective way.

Let's use an example to demonstrate how the vendor manager's own experience may provide an inaccurate measurement of the vendor's true performance. Assume that an organization has just outsourced a new function, such as health and welfare administration, that had previously been performed on a decentralized basis throughout the company. A new vendor management function has been established, and a vendor manager has been appointed. The provider's service center opens on January 1 and begins to handle 200 calls per day from plan participants. Not surprisingly, the newly trained team is making a certain number of mistakes, but it begins to improve quickly. At the same time, the HR generalists in the field begin to hear about some of the errors and to seek ways to assist employees in getting their problems resolved. So the HR generalists reach out and discover that a new vendor manager has been established whose job it is to help resolve escalated issues. The identity of that vendor manager slowly percolates among the employees of the company until eventually everyone in the organization knows whom they can call for help. This gradual knowledge about the existence of the vendor manager can be called vendor manager penetration. This very common scenario is summarized in Table 16.2.

Table 16.2

Example: New Call Center Implementation

Week	Calls per Day	Vendor Error Rate (%)	Daily Errors (Calls per Day x Vendor Error Rate)	Vendor Manager Penetration (%)	Escalated Calls per Week (5 Days x Daily Errors x Vendor Manager Penetration)	Frequency of Calls Received by Vendor Manager
1	200	10	20	1	1.0	1 call per week
2	200	9	18	2	1.8	1 call every 3 days
3	200	8	16	4	3.2	1 call every other day
4	200	7	14	8	5.6	1 call per day
5	200	6	12	16	9.6	2 calls per day
6	200	5	10	32	16.0	3 calls per day

As shown in the hypothetical scenario summarized in Table 16.2, the vendor has significantly improved its performance. In fact, it has reduced its error rate by half, from 10 percent to just 5 percent, yet the number of escalated calls being received by the vendor manager has increase sixteenfold, from one call per week to more than three calls per day. Clearly, if the vendor manager relies purely on his or her own experience with escalated calls, he or she will have the impression that the vendor's performance is moving in the exact opposite direction and that some immediate action needs to be taken in response.

This phenomenon can be considered the vendor manager's paradox. In other words, the mere fact that the vendor manager is the point of contact for all vendor-related problems creates a situation in which that same individual receives a negatively biased perspective of the vendor's true performance. Vendor managers will always receive more data about problems, mistakes, and issues than they will about successful service delivery. So they can become discouraged, finding themselves continually reacting to the latest crisis with their vendors and receiving little positive feedback.

Establishing a Measurement Framework

There is only one way to avoid the insidious cycle of reactive vendor management described above. It is absolutely essential that outsourcing relationships be managed on an objective basis that recognizes all of the various dimensions of activity that the supplier performs. This technique is often referred to as the *balanced scorecard* approach.

In the balanced scorecard approach, the client and the provider agree on a set of metrics that the vendor will measure and report on periodically. The most common measuring period for performance metrics is monthly or quarterly. Typically, those metrics represent objective measures of performance, but it is possible to introduce certain subjective measures of performance, as well to create an even broader measure of the provider's performance. For example, many organizations supplement their objective performance measures by requiring their provider to perform a customer satisfaction survey. Such surveys can be directed at recent users of the provider's services by selecting survey recipients from the provider's call logs or from Internet transaction logs.

To achieve the goal of seeking a balanced appraisal of the provider's services, you should identify one or more metrics for all of the various dimensions of quality you want to measure. Many organizations begin to define service quality from an employee's vantage point. Surveys of users of outsourcing services have identified certain key characteristics that affect their satisfaction. Table 16.3 identifies various dimensions of quality that should be considered and that reflect the user's perspective in a balanced scorecard approach.

Table 16.3

Dimensions of Quality: The Employee's Perspective

Dimension	Description
Accessibility	The first driver of employee satisfaction is the ability to reach the service provider at the times and from the places the employee desires to use the service.
Timeliness	The second driver of employee satisfaction is the timeliness of the response. For inquiries, employees are looking for the answer to their questions now. For transactions, employees seek a reasonable timeframe for the completion of the activity.
Accuracy	Implicitly, all users of outsourcing services presume that their inquiries and transactions are processed accurately and that they receive correct information.
Employee satisfaction	This subjective measure is the real definition of success (i.e., if the users are pleased with the service, then implicitly the provider is supplying acceptable quality services).

However, as indicated above, there are other dimensions of the perceived quality of services from the plan sponsor's perspective. Those additional definitions may also deserve consideration in developing the balanced scorecard. Table 16.4 describes additional dimensions of quality from the sponsor's perspective.

Table 16.4

Dimensions of Quality: The Sponsor's Perspective

Dimension	Description
Control	This dimension measures the effectiveness of the vendor's controls related to administrative tasks (e.g., case tracking, financial reconciliations, or workflow management). It represents a holistic approach to measuring the vendor's performance on behalf of individual employees who may not express dissatisfaction.
Reliability	This dimension measures the vendor's performance against scheduled tasks, such as report production, interface file delivery, or maintenance of production schedules.
Responsiveness	This dimension measures the ability of the service provider to support the change management activities required by the sponsor of the relationship. Typically, this measure is associated with the speed of implementation of required change order activity.
Sponsor satisfaction	This dimension is another subjective measure of success, but it is gathered from the individuals who monitor or otherwise interact with the service provider relationship. Providers must be able to satisfy the needs of this constituency, as well as those of employees.

Note that the appropriate metrics for any specific vendor relationship may vary. For example, if the vendor is providing a set of services, such as benefits administration, that are highly visible to employees and that affect their perception of the organization, it may be appropriate to place more emphasis on the dimensions of quality that affect employee satisfaction. But another vendor relationship, such as trust administration, may primarily support corporate objectives. In that case, the dimensions of quality that affect sponsor satisfaction should be emphasized.

The balanced scorecard approach can be successful only if there is agreement among all parties—including both your own management team and the provider—so that the scorecard reflects a fair and accurate representation of the quality of the vendor's performance. And once such agreement is reached, it is essential that both sides focus on the periodic performance reports as the mutual definition of success and not fall into the habit of reacting to hearsay or the problem of the day. Therefore, it is worth investing the time to consider which dimensions of quality apply on a vendor-by-vendor basis to ensure that the measurements are deemed relevant and applicable rather than attempting to use a single common set of metrics across all of your vendor relationships.

Identifying Appropriate Metrics

Once you have identified the dimensions of quality that you want to measure, the next step is to identify specific performance measurements for each of those dimensions. Note that it is impractical to measure every service that a vendor performs. In addition, some items that you might otherwise like to measure may not lend themselves to effective measurement, usually because the vendor's systems and processes may not allow the vendor to isolate the desired measurement. Therefore, the process of identifying the specific measurements within the balanced scorecard requires some flexibility and creativity.

The most effective approach is to seek to identify one or two indicator measurements for each dimension of quality. Indicator measurements should be individual measurable events, such as a type of transaction that is representative of similar processes being performed by the vendor. For example, a vendor may perform twenty or thirty different types of transactions in performing a service with varying levels of complexity and length of time to complete. However, it should be possible to identify a handful of transactions that are representative of the entire list and then to focus measurements on just those transactions. Table 16.5 provides some examples of indicator measurements that can be used to capture data with respect to each of the dimensions of quality identified above.

Table 16.5

Sample Indicator Measurements

Quality Dimension	Description of Potential Indicators
Accessibility	Service center availability, measured as the percentage of time the service center is open for participant contact as a percentage of its scheduled operation (This measure would capture any downtime from power failures or telecommunication problems.)
	Systems availability, measured as the percentage of time the self-service applications are available as a percentage of the scheduled hours for those services
Timeliness	New hire kits, measured as the percentage of kits that are processed and distributed within 3 days of hire as a percentage of all new hire kits processed and distributed
	First contract resolution, measured as the percentage of inquiries that were resolved during the initial call, rather than requiring the establishment of a case to research the request
Accuracy	Audit of manual calculations, measured by the level of accuracy determined through the audit of each transaction
	Audit of automated transactions, measured through the audit of a limited number of transactions (e.g., 10 per quarter) from 2 to 3 processes selected by the client.
Employee satisfaction	Survey of 100 employees or participants who used the service center during the prior reporting period
Control	Case management, measured as the percentage of cases that are resolved within prescribed timeframes following establishment
	Work activities, measured as the percentage of workflows or similar transactions that are completed within prescribed timeframes
Reliability	Production timeliness, defined as the percentage of batch activities that were performed as scheduled on the monthly production calendar (e.g., interface files sent, reports generated)
Responsiveness	Percentage of sponsor-requested change orders implemented within the agreed-upon timeframes
Sponsor satisfaction	Survey of the vendor management team on an annual basis against predefined measures of satisfaction

Vendors often lament that they do not have the infrastructure or mechanisms required to provide reporting on some of the indicators identified in Table 16.5. However, some tricks of the trade may enable vendors to meet your reporting needs. For example, many vendors will argue that they do not have an automated method for monitoring whether their systems or service centers are up and running. However, failures in either of those two tend to be infrequent, so it is a simple matter for the vendors to log the times that the systems are down or that power is out. The manual logs of downtime can then be compared against the expected hours of operation to determine the necessary statistics.

In other areas, it may be necessary to carefully select indicator variables from the list of transactions that can be monitored and reported electronically. Or in the extreme case, the parties could agree to use manual sampling of transactions on a periodic basis to gather the operating statistics. When discussing the desired level of reporting with your vendor, you could point out that, in the absence of objective data, your organization will be forced to rely on hearsay, which is a negatively biased set of data, to evaluate performance.

A service level agreement is the name for the document that summarizes the performance metrics that have agreed upon as representative of the balanced scorecard approach. In Box 4.1, we provided a sample of a service level agreement for benefits administration. That sample document provides measures for most of the dimensions of quality described in this chapter as well as examples of measurements that can be used to determine performance penalties.

Designing Performance Reports

There is also an art to designing performance reports. In particular, it is easy to make the mistake of producing so much data and information that the report is overwhelming. Producing too much data will have the inadvertent result that the reports will not be widely read; instead management will tend to fall back on relying on hearsay. Therefore, it is important to design a performance report in such a way that the information is quickly absorbed and that the service anomalies are readily identified. Behind this summary of the performance data, there may need to be reams of detailed information that supports the measurements. All of the data, however, need not be disseminated on a monthly basis.

It is also helpful to provide a historical record for the performance data for the prior twelve months. Many HR activities are cyclical, so volumes of activity may be unusual in certain months. Those unusual volumes may create service level anomalies that are temporary rather than representative of underlying service problems.

In addition, trends in the performance data can provide early warning signals of a potential degradation in service before performance penalty levels are reached. Or erratic performance may signal instability or inconsistency, which may also portend potential performance problems. For all of those reasons, performance reports should provide both a current and a historical summary of the information.

The best performance reports provide a quick summary of the following data:

- Service levels for each of the performance standards for the current reporting period

- Comparative statistics for each of the service levels for the prior twelve months

- Key volume statistics for the prior twelve months

Presented together, such reports provide a holistic picture of the provider's performance.

CHAPTER 17

Writing an Administrative Services Agreement

Many texts on outsourcing refer to the strategic partnership that is established between the buyer and seller of outsourcing services. Although one objective of any outsourcing relationship is to establish such a partnership, the basic foundation of that same relationship is a contractual business agreement. A healthy outsourcing partnership requires a mutual and unequivocal understanding of the objectives for the relationship. The document that captures and codifies this relationship is the outsourcing contract, usually referred to as an administrative services agreement.

Deciding Which Form to Use

One of the first decisions that a buyer of outsourcing services should make is which form of agreement to use: the one developed by the buyer or the standard contract provided by the seller. For smaller outsourcing relationships, or for situations in which the buyer has limited leverage, it is common practice to use the agreement supplied by the provider of services. However, for larger or more complex outsourcing arrangements, it is relatively common to start with a base agreement that was drafted by internal or external counsel and that represents the buyer of the services. In the most complicated outsourcing engagements, such as those supporting either services provided in multiple countries or those involving the transfer of staff members or physical assets under a business process outsourcing relationship, it may be necessary to draft a relatively complex agreement that has been customized for the specifics of the business relationship.

A sample administrative services agreement that might be appropriate for an outsourcing engagement covering a single HR function within the domestic United States, such as health and welfare benefits administration, has been included in the accompanying CD-ROM.

Organizing Attachments

The easiest way to organize an administrative services agreement for its initial negotiation, as well as for its use during the term of the outsourcing relationship, is to make effective use of exhibits rather than incorporating every aspect of the relationship in the main text of the contract itself. Ideally, the business aspects of the relationship would be captured in a series of schedules, which can be incorporated by reference into the contract. This approach allows the purchaser of the services to iron out the details of the outsourcing partnership while the legal and procurement teams resolve the more technical concerns of each organization.

The appropriate integration of the request for proposal, the vendor's fee proposal, and the contract was illustrated in Figure 6.1. As shown, you can design your RFP documents in a modular fashion that will allow you to incorporate those modules, as amended during your negotiations with the provider, into the agreement itself as exhibits that codify the business relationship that has been negotiated.

In addition, a few other aspects of any outsourcing relationship tend to lend themselves toward description in an exhibit rather than within the actual terms and conditions. Table 17.1 provides a listing and description of the exhibits that are commonly attached to an outsourcing agreement.

Examining Common Agreement Provisions

Not surprisingly, most outsourcing agreements address a common set of issues and concerns. The relative importance of the various issues

Table 17.1

Common Outsourcing Contract Exhibits

Dimension	Description
Statement of work	The most important exhibit to any outsourcing agreement-the statement of work-specifies the services, or business requirements, that the provider must perform. Ideally, it also specifies performance expectations for every aspect of the services. The statement of work is sometimes called a *service delivery model.*
Schedule of fees	This exhibit contains all of the financial provisions of the relationship, including the base fees, any transaction fees, and a description of pass-through expenses. It is also a good place to describe inflation adjustment provisions and invoicing requirements. Sometimes early termination penalties are also contained in this exhibit.
Service level agreement	This exhibit contains a description of all performance reporting, a definition of all performance measures, and a calculation of any performance standards and financial penalties.
Change order process	This exhibit describes the process for requesting and approving change orders. Change order rates may be specified in this exhibit, and it is often useful to attach a sample of the change request form.
Acceptance testing requirements	This exhibit specifies certain expectations and requirements that the provider must fulfill to be allowed to commence providing new services. The exhibit is useful for documenting in advance the acceptance test criteria that will be required to demonstrate the vendor's readiness to commence such services.
Transition assistance services	This exhibit describes the roles and responsibilities of the provider on termination or expiration of the agreement. The exhibit can also be used to describe whether such assistance is a normal in scope activity or whether it requires supplemental fees.
Disaster recovery and business continuation	The provider's disaster recovery and business continuation plans should usually be negotiated as a separate exhibit that is reviewed by the buyer's IT department without requiring its participation in the remainder of the negotiations.
Records retention policy	This is another good exhibit for protecting the buyer's interests on termination or expiration of the agreement. There should be explicit agreement with respect to the handling, storage, and disposal of all electronic and paper records.
Offshoring provisions	Offshoring introduces certain risks and concerns that may not exist for services provided using domestic resources. This exhibit allows the provider to separately describe and address those concerns. See Chapter 21 for more information on this topic.

depends on a host of factors, including the size of the relationship, its visibility to employees or customers, and any specific concerns of the organization establishing the relationship. However, it is possible to identify most of the major issues that should at least be considered, if not explicitly addressed, in any outsourcing agreement. Table 17.2 enumerates the key provisions that should be contained in most outsourcing agreements, as well as some comments with respect to the optimal resolution of those issues from the buyer's perspective.

Table 17.2
Summary of Common Terms and Provisions

Term	Description	Comments
Term	This provision defines the length of the agreement with the provider.	Most outsourcing agreements range from 3 to 7 years. This length of time seems to appropriately balance the large investment required to implement services with the loss of leverage associated with a long-term contractual relationship.
Renewal	This provision allows the buyer to renew the contract under certain agreed-upon terms at the end of this contract.	This provision is worth having in the contract to ensure that the buyer has at least one option available at the end of the term of the contract to continue administration. The buyer can always choose to renegotiate with the vendor or to rebid the work at that time rather than to use this provision.
Extension	This provision allows the buyer to extend the contract unilaterally for sufficient time to transition the services if an agreement cannot be reached on renewal or if the contract is being allowed to expire.	This valuable provision ensures that there isn't any sharp ending to the contract that could limit the buyer's options at the end of the initial term. Instead, the buyer would have the option to extend the contract for up to 12 months to facilitate a smooth transition.
Acceptance	This provision says that the services cannot go into operation unless the buyer accepts that the implementation has been completed to its satisfaction	This provision is a good protection to have in the contract. Otherwise, the buyer is subject to the vendor's definition of readiness to commence services.

Negotiating Process and Strategy

Many outsourcing relationships start with a high degree of excitement shared by the buyer and the provider, only to become strained during the contract negotiation phase. It is possible to avoid this pitfall—and its detrimental effect on the partnership—by following certain best practices in conducting the negotiations process.

The first step toward ensuring a smooth and effective contracting process is to resolve the vast majority of business issues as part of the selection process. In Table 17.1, we identified a number of contractual exhibits that will be required to clearly define the relationship with the service provider. Ideally, the business issues contained in the exhibits would have been resolved at a very specific level during the due diligence phase of the vendor selection process (see Chapter 7). However, if there are still lingering issues with respect to the scope of services required, the service level agreements, or the volume and pricing assumptions, those issues should be resolved before you commence with the negotiation of the agreement itself. In addition, you and the vendor should have resolved any key legal provisions at a conceptual level as part of the selection decision, including any limitations on liability or early termination provisions.

The best practice following the identification of the preferred vendor is to start contract negotiations immediately. Every day of separation between the vendor selection decision and the commencement of contract negotiations increases the probability that there will be difficulties in codifying the relationship in the administrative services agreement. It is imperative that you and the vendor commence work on the agreement while all of the compromises and promises you both have made are fresh and while there is still the opportunity to reset management expectations within either organization should an unanticipated point of disagreement arise.

The negotiation discussions themselves need to be disciplined and effective. In today's typical corporation, three or four parties are involved in most outsourcing negotiations: (a) the HR department (i.e., the buyer), (b) the legal counsel, (c) the purchasing or procurement department, and sometimes (d) an external consultant or advisor. Not surprisingly, it is easy to allow responsibility for controlling the process to become dispersed, thus resulting in a slow and ineffectual process. To prevent this mistake, you must establish clear roles and responsibilities for each of the parties. Three different approaches are commonly used. Those approaches can be equally effective, depending on the scope and complexity of the assignment in conjunction with the role procurement desires to play. The approaches are described in Table 17.3.

Note that it tends to be advantageous to the buyer to have either an external advisor or the procurement department in the lead in most negotiation situations, particularly those involving larger outsourcing relationships. Such an arrangement is advantageous for several reasons. First, it allows the HR staff to be focused primarily on preparing for the transition of the services to the provider. Second, it removes the HR representative one-half step from the negotiations so that the resolution of any difficult issues cannot damage the interpersonal relationship between HR and the provider. In instances in which the legal staff takes the lead, it is important that business aspects of the agreement still be represented by either HR or its external advisor. Regardless of the method used to lead the negotiations, it is essential for the HR staff to be engaged in the contracting process and to remain familiar with the resolution of all of the provisions during the process.

Finally, we would note that patience is definitely a virtue in a contract negotiations process. Although it is in both parties best interests to resolve issues as expeditiously as possible, sometimes issues arise that are difficult to resolve. Those issues do not necessarily represent a significant difference of position between the parties. Sometimes, it is merely difficult and time consuming to gain the necessary internal approvals to reach a compromise. Other times, issues will surface in the contracting process that will truly represent a misunderstanding or miscommunication between the parties. In those cases, it is not useful to invest time and energy debating what each party thought had been agreed on. Instead, it becomes necessary to revisit and resolve such issues in the context of reaching final agreement between the two organizations.

Table 17.3

Relative Roles and Responsibilities

Party Involved	Small Assignment with HR in Lead	Large Assignment with Advisor in Lead	Large Assignment with Procurement in Lead
Human resources	Performs overall scheduling Acts as primary negotiator Controls business exhibits	Resolves business issues	Resolves business issues
External advisor	If included, acts as advisor to human resources	Performs overall scheduling Acts as primary negotiator Controls business exhibits	Acts as advisor to human resources and procurement
Legal counsel	Controls administrative services agreement Controls nonbusiness exhibits Identifies general and specific legal issues	Controls administrative services agreement Controls nonbusiness exhibits Identifies general and specific legal issues	Controls administrative services agreement Identifies general and specific legal issues
Procurement	Acts as requested by human resources	Acts as advisor to human resources Ensures compliance with internal procurement policies	Performs overall scheduling Acts as primary negotiator Controls all exhibits

Designing Termination for Convenience, Expiration, and Renewal Provisions

One area of contracting that deserves special attention and is often overlooked is the way in which the agreement may be terminated or otherwise expire. Several scenarios are possible. Although contracts codify the ongoing relationship between the purchaser and the provider, one of the most common times they are referenced is when one of the parties wants to leave the relationship. It is easy to ignore this potential event in the excitement of the selection decision and the desire to complete the contracting process quickly. However, documenting the buyer's rights and protections and the provisions that will apply on termination or expiration of the agreement is very important. Dealing with those issues up front can prevent more contentious negotiations later.

In particular, these concerns should be addressed:

The buyer's right to terminate the contract early. In many cases, this right may be subject to the payment of an early termination penalty, but all organizations need to retain the right to terminate the agreement before it expires.

The buyer's flexibility at the expiration or termination of the agreement. Most outsourcing agreements are for a specific term, and they terminate on a specific date. Although this approach makes sense generally, it provides for little flexibility at the conclusion of the agreement. Buyers may want to explore providing for a short extension or renewal of the agreement at their sole discretion to allow additional flexibility under those circumstances.

The buyer's intellectual property rights at the expiration or termination of the agreement. Once services have been outsourced, much of the knowledge necessary to sustain the programs or to transfer them to a replacement provider will be transferred to the provider and documented in a set of requirements and desk procedures. Ownership of—or at least access to—those materials is an essential right that buyers should secure.

The provider's responsibilities at the completion of the agreement. The provider may need to return electronic or paper records, cooperate with the transition of services to the replacement provider, or provide special assistance during some part of the period of transition. Both the services and the manner in which the cost of those transition services will be determined should be resolved as part of the agreement.

CHAPTER 18

Managing a Proactive Governance Function

Establishing a Governance Structure

As described in Chapter 2, outsourcing relationships usually reflect a strategic decision to transfer responsibility for a significant function to an external entity. In other words, the buyer of the outsourcing services has reached the decision that the services being outsourcing are not essential to supporting the core value of the firm. Instead, the buyer hopes to be able to focus more of its resources and attention on its core values by transferring the management and operating responsibilities for the outsourced services to another organization. Note that though the buyer desires to transfer responsibility to the provider, it still retains accountability for the function. The process of monitoring and managing the vendor's performance as part of retaining functional accountability is called *governance*.

The outsourcing strategy will be successful only to the extent that the outsourcing organization can maintain acceptable levels of quality and cost, because otherwise the buyer will need to invest too much time and attention to the outsourcing relationship to make that relationship worthwhile. This symbiotic relationship between the buyer and provider of outsourcing services needs to be maintained throughout the term of the outsourcing relationship. The most effective way to ensure the continued strategic alignment between the two organizations is through proactive governance of the relationship by the buyer.

Vendor governance requires a tiered approach that reflects all of the various dimensions of the relationship. At the strategic level, there generally needs to be some type of executive steering committee. At the more tactical day-to-day level, a vendor management function must be in place. This chapter describes generally accepted best practices for establishing and designing this two-tiered vendor governance approach.

Table 18.1 describes the relative roles and responsibilities of the steering committee and the vendor management team as they relate to the overall management of the outsourcing relationship.

Table 18.1
Vendor Governance Roles and Responsibilities

Aspect of the Relationship	Steering Committee	Vendor Management Team
Strategic objectives	Maintains executive-level line of communication	Maintains functional-level line of communication
	Defines and communicates corporate objectives	Manages relationship to achieve corporate objectives
Quality of performance	Periodically reviews performance to ensure consistency with expectations	Monitors day-to-day performance
		Oversees performance improvement plans
Change management	Defines and communicates relative priorities	Manages internal development and communication to vendor of change requests
	Defines transformation and improvement objectives	Reviews and approves change orders
		Monitors project management of change order activity
Issue and dispute resolution	Resolves relationship disputes	Resolves escalated issues
		Oversees vendor escalation process
		Raises disputes to steering committee

Establishing the Role of the Steering Committee

The primary purpose of the steering committee is to periodically reinforce or refine the strategic objectives of the relationship. The composition of the steering committee is often defined in the administrative services agreement between the buyer and the provider.

Typically, the steering committee would consist of the executive sponsors of both organizations—that is, the individuals who were involved in the establishment of the relationship—plus the individuals who manage the relationship from day to day.

The objective of establishing this high-level governance team is to ensure the health of the strategic partnership at arm's length from the daily issues and concerns that will typically arise in an outsourcing relationship. As indicated at the beginning of Chapter 16, there are usually different objectives for the relationship at the corporate level than may exist at the functional level, where the work is performed. The steering committee is responsible for ensuring the ongoing balancing of those strategic objectives against the more tactical day-to-day concerns.

Steering committee meetings should be scheduled in advance on a periodic basis. For simpler relationships, an annual meeting may be sufficient. For complex relationships, more frequent oversight meetings may be appropriate. One advantage of prescheduled steering committee meetings is that they tend to defuse emerging issues between the organizations. Setting up a special meeting to discuss a problem or concern tends to escalate the importance of the problem, whereas merely assigning that same problem to the next steering committee agenda tends to allow it to be discussed and resolved in a more productive context.

The agenda for a typical steering committee meeting is a review of the vendor's performance, both qualitatively and financially. This review should be performed at a high level to set a baseline with respect to whether the vendor is meeting the general expectations for the relationship. The second part of the agenda is potentially more important and consists of a review of the change management objectives that have been achieved or are anticipated. Outsourcing relationships are seldom static; it is the vendor's ability either to facilitate required changes or to make enhancements to the services in a timely manner that will dictate most buyers' long-term satisfaction with the relationship. Therefore, sufficient time should be set aside in the steering committee agenda to allow the executives to reach an understanding of the evolving expectations for the vendor as a result of changes in the buyer's organization.

Building a Vendor Management Team

The next tier of the governance function that needs to be established is the vendor management team. The size and structure of the vendor management team depends on the size and complexity of the outsourcing relationship. A useful rule of thumb is that the vendor management function will cost about 5 to 10 percent of the annual fees of the outsourcing vendor. So, for example, the cost of managing a $2 million annual outsourcing relationship will be about $100,000 to $200,000 per year, thus suggesting a team of one to three staff members.

Because the size of a vendor management function will vary from vendor to vendor, it is helpful to use a role-based model when designing vendor management teams or considering how to allocate responsibilities among staff members who are already monitoring multiple vendor relationships. The role-based approach tends to be more flexible because it can accommodate the varying sizes of outsourcing relationships or even the varying needs of a single relationship from year to year.

Table 18.2 illustrates a simple role-based model that can be applied against most outsourcing relationships. For smaller outsourcing relationships, two or more of those roles may be performed by a single individual. For larger outsourcing relationships, each of the roles may require a different individual—or possibly even a team of individuals—to fulfill the requirements of the role.

Generally, buyers should exercise caution when assigning multiple roles to the same individual. There are two very different types of work—and, hence, different types of skills—required to manage an outsourcing relationship: (a) an operational role related to the day-to-day oversight of the relationship and (b) a change management role related to implementation of new services, acquisition and divestiture activity, and special program requirements. The two roles are inherently in conflict and ideally should be kept separate, because combining them could cause the performance of one of the two roles to degrade.

One common mistake many organizations make when designing their vendor management teams is to allocate responsibilities internally and then to ask the provider to match this internal structure.

Table 18.2

Roles and Responsibilities of the Vendor Management Team

Role of Team Member	Description of Responsibilities
Relationship management	Serves as primary contact for the vendor to communicate issues and concerns with respect to the business relationship between the firms
	Serves as the sponsor of the vendor within the buyer's organization
	Serves as the final point for escalation of issues before bringing them to the attention of the steering committee
	Coordinates and prioritizes all action planning by the vendor management team
	Monitors contract requirements, including maintenance of the statement of work
Delivery oversight	Monitors and evaluates vendor's performance through periodic reporting mechanisms
	Oversees vendor's development and implementation of action planning for making service delivery improvements
	Monitors escalated case log and coordinates internal resolution of issues, as may be required
	Maintains issues log with respect to service and relationship issues with the vendor
Change oversight	Develops change order requests, including detailed descriptions of the requested changes
	Facilitates review of vendor's draft change orders, works with vendor to identify appropriate solutions, and coordinates development and refinement of requirements
	Oversees and coordinates support of vendor's change implementation process, including project planning and acceptance testing
	Tracks status of all outstanding change order requests and other service implementation priorities
Data oversight	Monitors the delivery of data interfaces to and from the vendor
	Reviews control totals and error reports produced by the vendor
	Facilitates resolution of errors that require internal support
	Provides testing as may be required relative to interfaces affected by change management activities

In practice, this approach will ensure a suboptimal client–vendor relationship. It is actually much more effective to approach the vendor management design equation from the other direction by seeking to mirror your provider's structure and communication requirements.

You must recognize that the outsourcing provider is a large organization itself, even though your particular client team may be a small group of individuals. The vendor that your team works for has made its own specific decisions with respect to how to provide the services through some combination of technology, dedicated resources, and shared resources. This operating model is essential to the vendor's effective provision of services.

To maximize the utility of the model, your organization should understand how the provider desires to interface with you, and you should organize accordingly. After all, it is much simpler for your organization to restructure a small vendor management team than it is for your vendor to reorganize its thousands of employees. In the end, this commonality of client–vendor responsibilities and mirrored organizational structure will facilitate optimal communication and will provide an environment that maximizes the probability of the vendor's achieving successful results.

Monitoring Vendor Performance

One of the key functions of the vendor management team is to monitor the vendor's performance. Most of the responsibility for this activity falls under the delivery oversight role described in Table 18.2. A proactive schedule for monitoring service quality is, in most cases, essential if you are to avoid reacting to hearsay and are to maintain any semblance of control over the outsourcing relationship. Therefore, you must establish a plan for continuous service delivery evaluation and validation that is balanced across the entire spectrum of the vendor's operations.

Table 18.3 provides a sample vendor performance evaluation plan, including descriptions of certain activities that might be performed to assess various aspects of the vendor's performance. This plan can be adapted to any specific outsourcing relationship by changing the emphasis or frequency of the various activities that have been identified.

Table 18.3
Vendor Performance Monitoring Plan

Process	Description	Objective	Frequency
Call sampling	Make random calls into the service center to test center availability and speed of answer.	To certify the reasonableness of the vendor's reporting and to monitor the effect of ongoing turnover within the customer service staff	Perform on an ad hoc basis, as well as in conjunction with the implementation of any changes that will affect call volumes.
Call monitoring	Use the vendor's monitoring process to test call quality and representative skills. Mimic the vendor's procedure for evaluating call quality.	To provide a means for confirming the vendor's results in the area of call-handling quality To compile the results in a format that allows for a quantitative comparison and calibration with the vendor's own results	Perform jointly with the vendor on a regularly scheduled basis, at least monthly. Additional monitoring may be warranted if performance results have slipped or if significant features have been added or changed.
Participant correspondence review	Randomly sample and review correspondence being sent out of the service center.	To ensure that correspondence is being sent on a timely basis and that the information provided is accurate	Perform during randomly selected periods, depending on level of backlog.
Case log review	Regularly review open case logs to test the response time and the accuracy of the response.	To ensure that the timeliness and accuracy of case handling is acceptable	Perform periodically, depending on level of backlog.
Transaction sampling	Review an audited sample of the vendor's processed transactions.	To ensure the accuracy of the transactions being processed by the provider	Perform monthly, varying the transactions being sampled each month.
Monitor processing calendar	Review the vendor's schedule of processes to be performed in the timely administration of the required services.	To ensure that the vendor is performing its administration in accordance with its processing calendar	Perform in accordance with the vendor's schedule. The vendor should prepare the processing schedule on a monthly basis and should provide the status of processing no more frequently than weekly.

In addition, the vendor management team should schedule a periodic audit of the vendor's operating environment. The purpose of this audit is to go to the vendor's location to observe and monitor activities and processes that may require on-site monitoring or direct interaction with members of the vendor's staff. Table 18.4 describes some of the activities that might typically be performed during an audit of the vendor's service center.

Managing Change Order Activity

One of the aspects of vendor governance that many vendor managers find most challenging is managing change order activity. A *change order* is the method by which services are added, deleted, or modified in an outsourcing relationship. A change order usually starts with a request by the buyer of outsourcing services for some type of change. The vendor responds with an estimate of the cost to implement the change, plus an estimate of the effect that the change will have on the ongoing fees once it has been completed. This series of events related to the addition, modification, or deletion of a requirement under the outsourcing agreement is often referred to as the *change control process*.

Many vendor managers worry that the fees they are being charged to implement changes in the services being delivered either are too high or are unsupported. This concern usually arises because the buyer does not have an adequate understanding of how the vendor developed the cost estimate. As a result, both parties of most outsourcing relationships spend a lot of effort estimating and negotiating change orders.

Some ways of managing the cost of change order activity are more productive than debating each cost estimate developed by the provider:

Require documentation for change order estimates. Each change order estimate should be accompanied with documentation of the development of the fees in the form of estimated hours worked—by position and billable rate—for each phase of the implementation, including requirements definition, applications development, user acceptance testing, and training. Although no two change requests are likely to be identical, over time the vendor manager can develop some intuition with respect to the reasonableness of the change order estimates relative to prior estimates.

Table 18.4

Audit Activities during a Vendor Site Visit

Process	Description	Objective	Recommended Frequency
Review performance reporting tools	Ensure that the vendor is using appropriate tools for measuring each performance standard and that those tools are calibrated properly.	To ensure that the vendor has the proper means from which to determine performance results and to fully understand how the data are being compiled (Periodic reviews are necessary to make sure that the tracking tools are maintained accurately.)	Semiannually
Verify control mechanisms	Randomly select the review of audit and control documentation from various processes and transactions performed by vendor.	To ensure that standard audit and control procedures are being performed in a timely and effective manner, including management review and signoff	Quarterly
Validate manual processes	Randomly select the review of manually processed transactions to ensure that the vendor is processing transactions and other activity using standard audit and control procedures in a timely and effective manner, including management review and signoff.	To ensure that manual processes are being performed using agreed-upon desk and control procedures to guarantee the accuracy of the processing	Quarterly
Review infrequent processes	Review the process and procedure documentation for less frequent processes, such as annual tax reporting of information on Forms W2 and 1099R.	To ensure the preparedness of the vendor to manage those activities that are infrequent and are outside the standard set of activities performed on a day-to-day basis	As needed

Negotiate the solution rather than the price. Often, the initial estimate for the change will be based on the first solution that the vendor identified. Rather than argue about the price for that solution, it is often more fruitful to work with the vendor to consider alternative ways to implement the change that may be more cost-effective. Vendors will typically design their original solution in accordance with the most comprehensive way to implement the change, but other solutions may be just as satisfactory, particularly for any changes that are temporary in nature.

In the end, it is unlikely that vendor managers will ever have the level of control that they desire over their organization's change order fees and expenses. However, there is some empirical evidence with respect to the marketplace norms for the level of change order activity for different services. In 2002, the Human Resources Outsourcing Forum initiated a research project with the objective of developing some empirical data with respect to change order practices and norms in the benefits outsourcing marketplace. That research is an ongoing effort supported by nearly forty large companies with benefit outsourcing relationships.

Figure 18.1 illustrates the median level of change order activity as a percentage of outsourcing fees for three human resources functions: defined benefit, defined contribution, and health and welfare administration. As illustrated, the cost of change order activity tends to run between 5 and 12 percent when it is calculated as a percentage of the total cost of outsourcing service delivery. Note that a significant proportion of change order fees in benefits administration is related to the cost of implementing plan design changes or the expense in assimilating mergers and acquisitions. Therefore, organizations without any extraneous activity of those types should expect to incur significantly lower levels of change order fees than those shown in Figure 18.1.

Figure 18.1
Change Orders as a Percentage of Total Fees

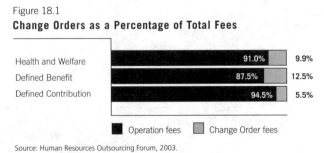

Source: Human Resources Outsourcing Forum, 2003.

The Human Resources Outsourcing Forum has plans to expand this research into all of the other functional areas within human resources as those outsourcing markets mature. In the meantime, the statistics from the benefits administration marketplace provide some useful barometers of the likely level of change order activity that may arise under other types of outsourcing relationships.

Benchmarking Services and Fees

Outsourcing relationships are typically codified under the assumption that the client organization's requirements will be static. In practice, most large organizations are constantly evolving as a result of one of the following factors:

- Growth or shrinkage in their core businesses

- Acquisition, merger, or divestiture activity

- Outsourcing or restructuring of current functions

It is difficult to design and negotiate provisions in outsourcing agreements that take into account the myriad ways that an organization may change over the term of a contract. In addition, the outsourcing market itself is constantly changing, with new services being introduced and with continuous pressure to reduce the fees charged for the services. Therefore, it is a good idea to periodically review the status of an outsourcing relationship and to benchmark it against current marketplace norms. At the least, benchmarking should be performed whenever an outsourcing relationship is renewed or whenever the size or structure of the organization changes so that there is a 10 to 15 percent increase or decrease in the number of employees being covered under the agreement.

It is useful to benchmark both the services and the fees under the outsourcing relationship. Most organizations limit their benchmarking activities to the cost of their outsourcing relationship. But new services are always being introduced and generally are implicitly reflected in the market-standard fee levels. Benchmarking both services and fees will ensure the accuracy of the conclusions reached about the reasonableness of the financial relationship.

Finally, we recommend that most organizations turn to an external advisor to assist them with a benchmarking exercise. There are many potential pitfalls in attempting to perform market benchmarking without experienced assistance. All of the following factors affect the range of fees that might be considered reasonable or market competitive: (a) size of the organization, (b) complexity of the services performed, (c) required service levels, and (d) any unusual or nonstandard services required. In addition, vendors use different methodologies for recovering their costs, including charging participants transaction fees, varying the treatment of pass-through expenses, subsidizing of fees through other services, and earning interest on float. In the end, benchmarking is a relatively complex exercise if one wants to have a reasonable degree of confidence in the conclusions reached.

Reviewing and Renewing Providers

The final area of significant responsibility for the vendor management function is the timely review and renewal of the outsourcing arrangement. The secret of a successful vendor renewal process is to start soon enough. Starting the process without sufficient time to make a replacement decision if your organization is unable to reach a satisfactory renewal agreement cedes too much negotiating leverage to the vendor. Thus, this situation should be avoided if at all possible.

To determine the correct time to start the renewal process, you merely need to work backward from the end of the outsourcing agreement. First, subtract the length of time that would be required to transfer the services to a replacement provider. Next, subtract the length of time that would be required to identify, select, and contract with a replacement provider. Finally, subtract a reasonable amount of time for the renewal negotiations—say two or three months. The result is the date on which renewal negotiations should commence. Figure 18.2 illustrates this process for the review of a defined contribution administration provider.

Figure 18.2

**Determination of Renewal Negotiations Commencement Date
for a Defined Contribution Administration Contract**

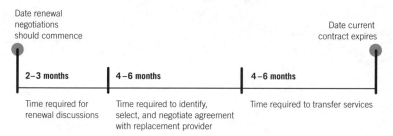

Date renewal
negotiations
should commence

Date current
contract expires

2–3 months	4–6 months	4–6 months
Time required for renewal discussions	Time required to identify, select, and negotiate agreement with replacement provider	Time required to transfer services

The typical conclusion drawn from this exercise is that renewal negotiations should start 12 to 18 months before the outsourcing agreement expires. Some organizations are uncomfortable commencing negotiations when so much time remains under the existing agreement. But vendor managers should remember that as part of the negotiation of a contract renewal it is possible to amend any and all of the provisions of the agreement, including the term. To the extent that the discussions lead to a renewal with the current provider, it is possible to merely subsume the final year of the current agreement into the renewal agreement. For markets with declining prices, this method may actually accelerate the buyer's ability to capture a better fee arrangement.

CHAPTER 19

Resolving Disputes and Terminating Vendor Contracts

In this final chapter on vendor management, we focus on tools and techniques to use when the outsourcing relationship is not meeting expectations with respect to service quality. Philosophically, it is important to approach this topic from the perspective that it is the vendor manager's role to assist the provider in improving its performance in accordance with the original objectives for the relationship. We have repeatedly emphasized that adopting outsourcing is a strategic decision by your organization and one that requires significant dislocation to implement. Reaching the decision to transfer outsourced services from one provider to another—or to reverse the original decision and bring such services back internally—also has significant ramifications and should not be considered lightly. It is often easier to invest some time and effort in revitalizing an existing outsourcing relationship rather than assuming that the grass will be greener under other circumstances.

Handling Escalated Case Management

One of the most common areas of frustration among vendor managers is their involvement in escalated case management. It is a common lament among vendor managers that they spend a disproportionate amount of their time helping vendors resolve individual participant issues, which are usually called *cases* in outsourcing. Worse yet, the sheer volume of cases that they are helping to resolve gives them a negative perspective of the vendor's performance.

Escalated cases arise in a number of ways. Some cases may be escalated from the outsourcing provider to the vendor manager for policy decisions. Others may require historical data research that precedes the vendor's engagement. But in many organizations, cases are created directly with the vendor manager when an employee, manager, or HR generalist within the organization is permitted to contact the vendor manager without having first contacted the outsourcing service provider. Allowing direct contact with the vendor manager is generally a mistake, with the one possible exception: executives may need to initiate cases directly through an internal mechanism.

Vendor managers should do everything possible to avoid getting directly involved in case resolution for many reasons. First, case management is a vendor responsibility. Sharing that responsibility with the vendor is likely to introduce questions about accountability. Second, case management is the single most common distraction that inhibits vendor managers' ability to proactively oversee their outsourcing relationships. As a practical matter, the sheer volume of case activity can absorb too much of a vendor manager's time, preventing other important vendor management activities, as described in Chapter 16, from being completed.

Extricating a vendor manager from case management activity requires significant discipline on the part of the vendor manager. In addition, the vendor may have to create a mechanism to ensure that certain cases get immediate attention. Creating a special classification of cases, called *hot cases*, that the vendor manager can select for accelerated resolution by the vendor may allow the vendor manager to concentrate on his or her real job responsibilities, because the accelerated treatment will ensure the rapid resolution of the hot issue.

Fixing Problems

Another common mistake that many vendor managers make is to dictate solutions to their outsourcing providers. The reason that this approach is often ineffectual is that it is possible the vendor manager is viewing only the ramifications of the mistake and may not be aware of the root cause of the problem.

Suppose, for example, that a vendor performing health and welfare administration has inadvertently coded a mistake in the programming of the eligibility interface file to one of its carriers and that the mistake affects a small group of part-time employees. Some of those employees—on being informed that they are ineligible for medical coverage—call the service center to inquire about their eligibility. The service center then compounds the error by incorrectly describing the plan's eligibility requirements. The vendor manager, on hearing tapes of the incorrect description of the plan's eligibility provisions, insists that the vendor immediately develop a new training module and provide refresher training to all of its customer service representatives about part-time employee eligibility.

The vendor, however, would like to have the same subject matter experts who are being asked to develop the training module to instead work with its programming staff to provide revised specifications to correct the file interface. After all, if the interface file were correct, the part-time employees would be eligible for medical coverage and would never call the service center to inquire about their eligibility provisions. In this example, the vendor manager has correctly identified a training gap; however, the vendor manager's prescriptive approach to how the problem is to be resolved will extend the length of time that the eligibility problem will exist. Eliminating the problem at its root cause and then performing the remedial training would actually be much faster.

The point of this example is that vendor managers should identify problems but then require their vendors to provide remediation action plans. Only the vendor will be in a position to accurately diagnose the root cause of many problems. Therefore, the best practice is to allow the vendor to propose the optimal solution to most problems.

Using the Seven Steps Model

Provider service quality challenges may seem so overwhelming that it is difficult to know where to start. Often, the result is that the client organization insists that the provider fix everything at once. This approach is usually either impractical or impossible from the vendor's perspective and merely leads to a further disconnect in the vendor's relationship with the client. In our experience, there is a more effective approach toward the revitalization of an outsourcing agreement that relies on a staging of the improvement efforts that is manageable and can be monitored for progress.

We call this approach the *seven steps model*. It is based on the concept of incremental improvement, with the initial emphasis on the most visible aspects of quality service and the later work on the more difficult aspects to improve, as the vendor's credibility is restored. The seven steps are described in sequential order in Table 19.1.

The key to the seven steps approach is to first try to take some of the noise out of the system by providing a reasonable level of service to employees. If your vendor can accomplish steps 1 through 4, then it will have significantly reduced the visibility of the underlying problems in the service center. The problems may still exist and require resolution, but a safety net will have been established around the individual employee interactions. This safety net will restrict the visibility of most problems to members of the vendor management team.

Once the external pressure created by the visibility of the problems has been relieved, the vendor can turn its attention to correcting its systems, implementing additional controls, or revising its processes to eradicate the basic underlying problems. But often system corrections are required in the final analysis, and such corrections take time to implement. Thus, it is critical that the vendor buy some time to make those changes by first addressing issues arising from individual employee interactions. Such issues can often be addressed merely by working longer hours or adding staff members on a temporary basis.

Terminating an Outsourcing Contract

There are two provisions for terminating an outsourcing agreement:

Termination for Convenience. Under this provision, the buyer of outsourcing services may terminate the agreement for any reason. However, to invoke this provision, the buyer usually is required to pay some type of early termination penalty to compensate the vendor for the unexpected termination of the agreement before the expected term of the agreement.

Table 19.1

Seven Steps Model as Applied to a Call Center

Step	Description
1. Get the calls.	Ensure that there is adequate staffing in the service center to answer all the calls within the expectations of performance that have been established. Fixing this problem merely requires a commitment by the provider to add staff members.
2. Handle the calls.	Work with the provider to improve its customer service training and online tools so customer service staff members can resolve the requests for information or action being received.
3. Close the cases.	Monitor that the provider is closing any outstanding cases as quickly as possible. Remember, a case is, by definition, an unsatisfied user of the services. Again, a commitment by the provider to add staff members will often enable the reduction of outstanding case volumes.
4. Get the work done.	Double-check that the provider is completing its processing as scheduled. Both individual transactions and batch processes should be checked. Delays in processing will merely result in more calls and more cases, thus causing a further degradation in perceived service levels.
A safety net has now been established. Note that the first four steps can largely be accomplished by adding resources or extending work hours. Accomplishing these first four steps will buy the provider time to make the more permanent corrections in the final three steps.	
5. Do the work right.	Ironically, improving the accuracy of the work can often be deferred, even under extreme circumstances. As long as the provider is quickly rectifying its errors, as reflected in steps 1 through 4, it will often gain the time required to make the systems, process, or control corrections required to eliminate processing errors.
6. Enhance the systems.	Often, it is necessary to implement manual workarounds or temporary processes once processing problems have been uncovered. The secret is then to convert those stopgaps into permanent solutions by correcting the underlying administrative systems.
7. Manage change.	Finally, implement the structured change management processes, including acceptance testing, that are required to ensure that new errors don't arise following changes to the services.

Termination for Default. Under this provision, the buyer may terminate the agreement because of some breach by the vendor. The most common type of breach that might result in a termination for default would be a breach of the vendor's warranty with respect to the quality of its services. Under this provision, the buyer can usually transition services away from the vendor without paying any penalty; instead, the vendor may actually either incur a penalty of its own or be required to assist the buyer in transitioning the services for free.

As a practical matter, it is often difficult to demonstrate that a vendor is in default of its obligations under an outsourcing agreement. Therefore, many organizations have been forced to use the termination for convenience provision even if they believe the vendor to be in default. In some cases, those same organizations have been able to negotiate a reduction of the early termination penalty in conjunction with the orderly transition of services to a replacement provider.

Some buyers have attempted to define specific circumstances that would be deemed to be a default by the provider or events that, though not a default per se, might create conditions under which the buyer might want to transfer the services to another provider. Examples of such conditions would include bankruptcy by the provider or its acquisition by a competitor of the buyer.

One method tends to be effective in establishing whether a vendor is, in fact, in breach of its service obligations while at the same time providing an opportunity to that same vendor to correct its service deficiencies. In particular, it is possible to work with the vendor to develop a mutually agreed-upon schedule of improvements, perhaps using the seven steps approach outlined above. As part of the agreement on the service remediation plan, the vendor will need to confirm that its inability to achieve the goals and objectives of the plan will be deemed a breach of the agreement, thus allowing the client to invoke the termination for default provisions. This approach reasonably balances the vendor's opportunity to regain the confidence of the client with the client's need to resolve the service problems one way or another.

Bringing Services Back in House

Few outsourcing relationships in the HR marketplace have been terminated for the purpose of bringing the services back in house. Instead, it is more common to transfer the services to a different outsourcing provider. The trend in most HR functions over the past two decades has been a steady increase in the use of outsourcing for most administrative delivery activities. Therefore, though emotionally one may want to regain control of the services by bringing them back in house, other external replacement options warrant equal time and consideration in most cases.

There may be, however, circumstances that might suggest that bringing the services back in house is the best alternative. In those instances, the process of reestablishing the services internally is the reverse of the original implementation to the outsourcing provider. Typically, a data and systems conversion will be required, followed by the hiring and training of an administrative delivery staff. The one difference is that much of the subject matter expertise required to successfully transition the services will now exist only at the vendor. Therefore, a key step in such a transition is securing the necessary support from the outsourcing vendor for the implementation process. Once that support has been secured, it is a matter of managing the implementation project successfully.

PART V

Considering Global Issues

CHAPTER 20

Incorporating Global Requirements

The techniques described in this book generally apply to most organizations. However, certain complexities can arise when establishing outsourcing relationships that cover activities in multiple countries. This chapter identifies those anomalies and introduces techniques that can be used to address the unique issues found in global outsourcing arrangements. Note that this chapter focuses on the extension of a domestic outsourcing relationship outside the United States. Readers interested in establishing outsourcing relationships in other countries can rely on the general principles as outlined in Chapters 1–8.

Examining Human Resources as a Multilocal Phenomenon

The HR function, perhaps more so than other corporate functions, varies significantly by country. Some experts like to describe human resources as a *multilocal activity*. This term is an excellent representation of the HR function, which tends to have its own characteristics and requirements within each country around the world. Obviously, there are language and cultural differences in most countries, but there are also more fundamental differences in common work practices that make a one-size-fits-all approach to outsourcing impractical.

For example, in the Netherlands, it is common for employers to have a bicycle policy, because bicycles are the most common mode of transportation. In India, many regions require employers to provide transportation to and from the office each day. In the United States, corporations typically provide health care benefits, yet in many countries around the world, health care is a service provided by the government. The list goes on and on, with significant variations in the relationship between the employee and employer, a relationship that is reflected in the services required of the HR function.

Simplistically, many organizations attempt to export outsourcing concepts and approaches that work in the United States to other countries. For example, it is tempting to consider establishing regional call centers in Europe and Asia that would provide employee and manager support on common policy issues. However, the multiplicity of language requirements often makes the concept of a shared services center impractical at best. So although the strategy of outsourcing can certainly be applied in any region of the world, it may need to be applied individually within each country, or else local differences need to be explicitly recognized in any cross-border outsourcing arrangements.

Understanding Legislative Challenges

Although many country-specific legislative issues affect outsourcing, two specific areas of law that are particularly important:

- Transfer of undertakings (protection of employment) regulations

- Data privacy legislation

Some countries in the European Union (EU) have legislative restrictions that affect outsourcing. Those restrictions were established by the European Acquired Rights Directive, the application of which is contained in regulations on the "Transfer of Undertakings (Protection of Employment)," or TUPE. TUPE entitles employees to continuation of pay, position, and benefits if their job (i.e., their "undertaking") is transferred. Depending on how work is being restructured as a result of the outsourcing, TUPE may apply. Hence, the provisions of TUPE should be reviewed in the context of any outsourcing in countries affected by TUPE legislation. A general rule of thumb when considering outsourcing in the EU is to assume that the regulations apply and to act accordingly, unless you can be assured of an exemption from their applicability. It is also a good idea to confer with legal counsel on this complex issue.

Data privacy regulation is an emerging area of legislation in almost every developed country in the world and is a well-established practice in Europe. Although in the United States data privacy legislation tends to focus on personal health care and financial data, in other countries around the world personal information is much more broadly protected and restricted by law. Such regulations present challenges in outsourcing relationships in which global databases are being established or employee support services are being provided outside the boundaries of the employee's country of residence. Even if the services have been contracted domestically, any use of offshoring by the domestic vendor can introduce questions of compliance with data privacy legislation. Again, legal counsel should review the provider's compliance with all relevant data privacy issues and concerns.

Other legislative challenges arise in specific countries as well. For example, services such as those provided by an outsourcing vendor would generate sales tax in certain countries. Needless to say, internal or external counsel should be engaged to review any unanticipated legislative challenges or risks associated with global outsourcing projects.

Looking at Variations by Geographic Regions

The most important variation by geographic region is arguably the difference in the employment relationship between companies and their employees in Europe. In particular, members of the EU are required to establish a structure and process for informing and consulting employees with respect to certain actions that are under consideration, including outsourcing. The requirements are contained in an EU directive (2002/14/EC) that applies to undertakings with at least fifty employees or establishments with at least twenty employees.

Most member states have implemented the directive by creating works councils. Works councils are standing bodies of elected employee representatives that provide a mechanism for worker involvement, consultation, and representation in decision making at the workplace. The EU directive does not specify the specific manner in which this representation must be implemented. However, works councils exist in some form in most nations in the European Union, except countries such as Ireland and the United Kingdom that have another system of employee representation (e.g., trade unions). Regardless of the specific form that such employee representation takes, employers are required to inform and gain the concurrence of the employee organization when implementing outsourcing arrangements in Europe.

In Asia, there are two significant challenges. The first challenge is the wide disparity in the languages that are spoken, particularly because this region does not generally recognize English as a second, or business, language as readily as it is adopted in Europe. The second challenge is the array of significant cultural differences not only between Eastern and Western civilizations, but also among China, Japan, South Korea, Thailand, and India. Those differences are much greater than among the EU countries, for example, and further complicate any efforts to establish regional delivery activities in the area.

Central and South America actually present some interesting opportunities from an outsourcing perspective. Although most South American countries have adopted Spanish or Portuguese as their primary language, many countries have historically had large populations from other countries and, therefore, have a labor force with diverse language skills. For example, the second greatest concentration of Japanese-speaking people in the world is in Brazil. Thus, Brazil is an excellent candidate for offshoring work for Japanese outsourcing organizations. Many domestic U.S. outsourcing organizations have already established service center locations in Central and South America, including not only Brazil, but also Costa Rica and Argentina.

Australia, with its English-speaking heritage, tends to have its own local outsourcing options, as found in Canada, the United Kingdom, and the United States. Meanwhile, there is very limited outsourcing activity today in Africa, although one provider has established a data processing facility in Ghana.

The variation of languages, currencies, and standard HR practices in countries outside the United States all need to be taken into account when developing a global outsourcing strategy. Table 20.1 summarizes some of the key factors that are likely to affect the design and implementation of a global outsourcing strategy for human resources.

Table 20.1

Key Factors Affecting Development of Global Strategy

Country	Primary Language(s)	Currency	Benefits	Work Councils or Equivalent
North and South America				
Brazil	Portuguese	Real	Employer-provided	No
Canada	English and French	Canadian dollar	Employer-provided	No
Mexico	Spanish	Mexican peso	Employer-provided	No
United States	English	U.S. dollar	Employer-provided	No
Europe				
Belgium	Dutch, French, and German	Euro	Government-provided	Yes
France	French	Euro	Government-provided	Yes
Germany	German	Euro	Government-provided	Yes
Italy	Italian	Euro	Government-provided	Yes
Netherlands	Dutch	Euro	Government-provided	Yes
Portugal	Portuguese	Euro	Government-provided	Yes
Spain	Castilian	Euro	Government-provided	Yes
Switzerland	German	Swiss franc	Employer-provided	No
United Kingdom	English	U.K. pound sterling	Government-provided	Yes
Asia and the Pacific				
Australia	English	Australian dollar	Government-provided	No
China	Chinese (Mandarin)	Yuan	Government-provided	No
India	English	Indian rupee	Government-provided	No
Japan	Japanese	Yen	Government-provided	No
Malaysia	Bahasa Melayu	Ringgit	Government-provided	No
Singapore	Chinese	Singapore dollar	Government-provided	No
South Korea	Korean	South Korean won	Employer-provided	No

Knowing Vendor Capabilities

Not surprisingly, there is a considerable amount of variation in capabilities within the domestic vendor community outside the United States. Some HR providers that have their roots in IT outsourcing have considerable experience operating in Asia and Europe. Other HR providers that are in the midst of expanding their services from U.S. benefits into broader HR services have very limited experience operating outside North America. Still other specialist providers, such as some of the large payroll providers, have been gradually expanding their footprint in their specific service areas into other countries.

It is difficult to generalize about the current state of international capabilities because they vary significantly by provider. However, it is easy to identify due diligence that should be undertaken when considering some kind of a global outsourcing relationship that includes services provided in multiple countries around the world. First, it is important to understand whether the specific functions under consideration will actually be performed outside the United States; the provider may have personnel in global locations, but those staff members may be performing other functions. Second, it is useful to understand whether the global location is performing services for that country locally or whether it is being used as an offshore location for services being provided in a different country. Finally, it is important to find out the size and significance of each global location. Many providers will list a presence in a given country but have only a single resource in that location.

Developing a Global Delivery Strategy

There are close to 200 countries in the world today. According to Ethnologue, which can be viewed at www.ethnologue.com, the more than 6 billion people in our world speak an estimated 6,900 different languages, including those that use nonroman symbols, such as Arabic, Chinese, and Japanese. Those two factors—the number of countries and the tremendous variety of languages—often seem to present an insurmountable barrier to developing an integrated global strategy for HR administration. But while there are challenges, there is hope that the outsourcing community will be able to deliver an integrated, scalable, global model for HR delivery that most large multinational organizations can use.

Recently, Fidelity Human Resources Services Company performed some very interesting research on the geographic distribution of the employees of large U.S. multinational organizations. Fidelity was interested in identifying those countries where U.S. multinationals had the largest concentrations of employees. The company conducted a survey that asked organizations to identify the three countries outside the United States where they had the largest concentrations of employees. Fidelity's research indicates that more than 80 percent of such non-U.S. sites are found in just sixteen countries. A summary of Fidelity's research is illustrated in Figure 20.1.

Figure 20.1

Percentage of U.S. Multinationals with Significant Presence

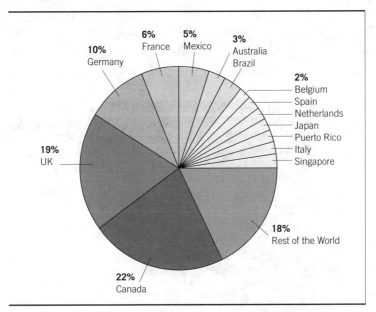

Note: Companies have between 430 and 750 employees on average per country.
Reprinted by permission of Fidelity Human Resources Services Company.

This research suggests that domestic outsourcing vendors can provide reasonable support for their clients' global needs. Outsourcing vendors will need some level of outsourcing services in about twenty countries—the ones listed in Figure 20.1—plus some strategically important emerging locations such as China, India, and Russia. Developing a solution for the rest of the world relies on an extension of the services in those key locations.

Although this expectation for the future capabilities of the vendor community is reasonable, it is interesting to compare this end-state objective to the kind of global coverage that is currently available from the outsourcing vendor community. Figure 20.2 summarizes the percentage of the seven leading domestic U.S. providers of outsourcing services that have locations providing HR services in twenty key countries around the world. Although there are certainly also local providers of HR services in each of those countries, Figure 20.2 provides some sense of an organization's ability to provide coverage around the world through a single outsourcing relationship with a global vendor. As you can see, the vendor community already has a reasonable global footprint in place today and can be expected to increase that footprint quickly as the market matures in the coming decade.

Figure 20.2
U.S. Outsourcing Providers with Locations Offering HR Services

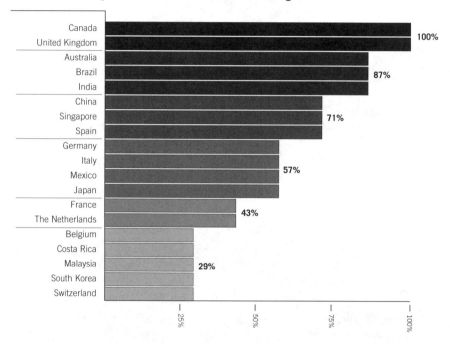

Seeing What Lies Ahead

We foresee the rapid expansion of vendor capabilities outside the United States. As large domestic organizations implement broad-based outsourcing of the HR function here in the United States, many of them are freeing up capital from the resulting savings, and some will elect to invest that capital in improving the global integration of their HR function. In addition, it seems likely that some of the competitors in the emerging HR outsourcing market will attempt to strategically differentiate their firms' ability to support organizations globally.

So although the services that are currently available are relatively limited, we would expect that the following capabilities will rapidly become more commonly available around the world:

- Maintenance of basic employee data on a consolidated and integrated basis

- Support for global workforce reporting and analytics

- Facilitation of common HR transactions, such as new hires, transfers, and terminations

- Local language support for employees and managers through self-service and shared service centers

- Integrated interfaces to third-party payroll and benefit providers in countries where the vendors do not offer those services themselves

- Global support for talent development, including compensation administration and performance management to assist multinational organizations in identifying and developing their talent across the globe.

These emerging capabilities will be attractive to organizations whose workforces are being redeployed around the world.

CHAPTER 21
Offshoring and Near-Shoring

Offshoring is defined as using resources outside of a country to perform services that have historically been performed by resources within that country. A common example today would be the growth of call centers in locations such as India or the Philippines to provide customer service support for U.S. consumers.

Near-shoring is a term for offshoring that is based on the geographic proximity of the offshore country. For example, establishing those same call centers in New Brunswick, Canada, rather than in India or the Philippines would be considered a near-shoring strategy.

This book is about outsourcing HR administration. Today's media often treat *offshoring* and *outsourcing* as synonymous terms. But offshoring and near-shoring are really tactics used by outsourcing organizations to gain a strategic advantage over their competitors or to provide a competitive value proposition for their customers. In other words, companies can outsource without offshoring, or they can offshore themselves without outsourcing. However, today's outsourcing providers are beginning to aggressively use offshore and near-shore resources in their service offerings. Therefore, it is essential for HR professionals to understand the potential effects of those strategies when making outsourcing decisions.

Labor Arbitrage

The original genesis of offshoring was a desire among corporations to capture the differences in labor rates among various countries. This process of having the same work performed by equally skilled employees in a country with lower rates of pay is often called labor arbitrage. Figure 21.1 illustrates the relative labor rates within several large countries. At a glance, the powerful attraction that labor arbitrage holds for organizations that can capture it to their advantage becomes apparent.

Figure 21.1
Comparative Direct Labor Rates: Average Rate for Entry-Level IT

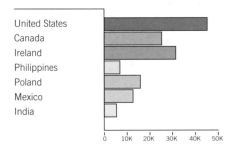

Source: neoIT, Global IT Salary Study, May 2005.

Note that Figure 21.1 also illustrates the attractiveness of various near-shore locations, such as Canada or Mexico relative to the United States. Similar labor cost differences exist between Ireland and the United Kingdom. Although the potential for labor arbitrage is much lower, the barriers to establishing such locations are also much easier to surmount, which makes near-shoring a simpler strategy for some organizations to adopt.

Other Factors

Many factors besides labor arbitrage affect the identification of potential offshore locations. The most obvious impediment to shifting services outside of one country is the potential for communication barriers if people in the offshore location do not speak the same language as people in the country from which the work is originating. For example, labor rates in China are very low relative to similar rates in the United States, but very few Chinese workers speak English. So China would be a poor candidate as a location for a call center to support U.S. workers.

Another important factor is the size of the relevant workforce within the country. For purposes of HR administration, not only language but also relative level of education would be an important consideration. Most countries with low labor rates also have low levels of education. However, there are some exceptions. India is perhaps the best example of a nation with low labor costs and yet a sophisticated education system. Although the education system may not provide a homogeneous level of education to all Indians, the university system in India does produce 2.5 million graduates a year. And in some areas, such as systems engineering, India produces more graduates than any other country in the world. In 2001, U.S. universities graduated 100,000 engineers and computer scientists, while Indian colleges produced more than 160,000 graduates with comparable degrees.

Figure 21.2 illustrates the relative attractiveness of the labor markets within several countries that are often considered as offshore locations. The placement of the countries is based on the relative attractiveness of those countries along two dimensions: total labor costs and the quality of the workforce, including not only the educational level and cultural compatibility, but also the size and availability of that workforce.

Figure 21.2
Relative Attractiveness of Labor Markets

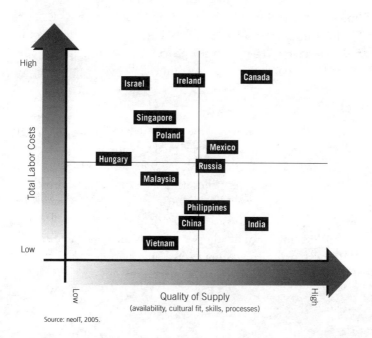

Source: neoIT, 2005.

Several other factors also may affect the relative attractiveness of various offshore or near-shore locations:

- Cultural compatibility of the offshore location

- Government stability and support of international commerce

- Existence of the required infrastructure, such as power and telecommunications

All of these factors should be considered when evaluating offshoring and near-shoring arrangements.

Assessment of Offshoring in Human Resources

Although the options seem virtually endless, it is possible to assess the potential effects of offshoring with respect to HR administration. In particular, it is possible to summarize those factors that are relevant to HR outsourcing to identify the countries that are the most likely to be attractive offshore locations for U.S. outsourcing organizations. Figure 21.3 illustrates a summary of six potential offshore locations against certain key criteria that would apply to HR administration. On review of this information, one quickly sees that the most likely locations for offshoring of HR functions are Canada, India, and the Philippines. Although specific functions within human resources may be offshored to other locations—for example, applications development to China or data entry to Indonesia—the services that require some level of interaction between the provider and the client are most likely to occur in one of those three countries.

Future of Offshoring

Offshoring was the topic of some emotional debate in the U.S. presidential election of 2004. Not surprisingly, many bills have been introduced—particularly at the state level, where the offshoring may affect local economies—to limit the offshoring of jobs. However, it is difficult to envision that such legislation can be enforced, even if it gains political momentum. Most U.S. corporations today already have employees in locations around the world. It is an impossible task to differentiate offshoring from other tasks being performed in nondomestic locations. So though local or state governments may place

Figure 21.3
Comparison of Potential Offshore Locations

	Canada	China	India	Ireland	Philippines	Russia
Government support	Medium	Low	High	High	Medium	Low
Labor pool	Medium	Low	High	Low	Medium	Low
Infrastructure	High	Medium	Medium	High	High	Low
Educational system	High	High	High	High	Medium	High
Cost advantage	Medium	High	High	Low	High	High
Quality	High	Low	High	High	High	Low
Cultural compatibility	High	Low	Medium	High	High	Low
Time–distance advantage	Low	High	High	Low	High	Medium
English proficiency	High	Low	High	High	High	Low

○ Low   ◐ Medium   ● High

Source: neoIT, Mapping Offshore Markets, April 2003

some restrictions on the work that is performed offshore for those organizations, we cannot imagine a scenario in the corporate marketplace that limits offshoring.

As organizations become more comfortable with using global resources to perform various HR activities, it is likely that additional benefits will begin to accrue to those organizations as has occurred in other industries. Workers in various countries are a byproduct of their education systems and cultures. And some countries produce workers that are better suited for various activities than others. For example, in India, most schoolchildren are continuously ranked in their classes, and those rankings are posted publicly. So Indian students become comfortable with their performance being monitored and published, and they become accustomed toward working to improve their relative position in the classroom. This cultural acceptance of measurement, comparison, and monitored improvement lends itself exceptionally well to HR transaction processing. Not surprisingly, most providers have found that the productivity of Indian workers is higher than that of their U.S. counterparts with respect to certain repetitive activities.

At the same time, experience among global workforces suggests that U.S. workers excel in creative and problem-solving pursuits relative to workers in more regimented societies. Hence, it seems likely that Americans will continue to be heavily involved in the design and development of new processes and techniques for delivering HR administration.

Effect of Outsourcing on Vendor Management

Offshoring presents some challenges for vendor management. First, some very practical issues arise from offshoring, including the difficulty of traveling to offshore locations to monitor activity; the differences in time zones, which may affect planning and scheduling; and the language and cultural barriers that can inhibit communications.

Perhaps more important, offshoring may create some risks that are not inherent in the use of a domestic workforce. Earlier in this chapter, we described a number of factors that providers need to consider when identifying their preferred offshore locations. Although the provider community may have resolved its own concerns relative to those issues, users of outsourcing may need to perform some of their own due diligence to become equally comfortable with the provider's use of offshore resources. For example, a provider may decide that the political risk in Malaysia is acceptable when it decides to establish a data entry facility in that country. But if there is political unrest in Malaysia that ends up affecting the services the provider is contracted to supply, it is the user of that provider's services that may suffer the service degradation.

The Human Resources Outsourcing Forum recently completed a detailed assessment of the risks of offshoring in HR outsourcing. The forum is an outsourcing user group whose membership consists of large corporations with significant HR outsourcing relationships. Forum members periodically meet to share best practices and to influence the evolution of the HR provider community. The forum sponsored a task force that conducted a yearlong analysis of the implications of offshoring, including interviews with service providers about their offshore strategies, meetings with the providers about their risk assessments, on-site reviews with provider staffs throughout India, and discussions with recognized consulting experts in offshoring. The task force identified the following areas of risk that apply to HR outsourcing; those risks should be reviewed as part of normal due diligence for a provider's offshore locations:

- Security

- Personnel and operations

- Work rules

- Change management

Table 21.1 contains a series of guidelines recently published by the Human Resources Outsourcing Forum that can be used as a starting point to ensure that an outsourcing provider has reasonably addressed those risks.

Ideally, providers using offshore facilities would offer some level of additional assurance that they have mitigated any incremental risks. Buyers of outsourcing should ensure that their agreements with suppliers include warranties related to some or all of those potential risks. Alternatively, such agreements should provide for gain sharing, whereby some of the savings from shifting services offshore is reflected in a reduced cost of the services. This approach will at least compensate the buyer for accepting the risks associated with offshoring.

Table 21.1

Guidelines for Offshore Locations

Number	Item	Guideline
1.0:	**Security**	
1.1	General	The site security should be reasonably acceptable to the client, as described in these requirements. The vendor should demonstrate that its security policies are in material compliance with BS 7799/ISO 17799 standards.
1.2	Physical	The work should be performed in a physically secure facility. Minimum physical security requirements include • Perimeter access deterrents, monitors, or alarms • Card access • Security guards • Security cameras and intrusion detection systems • Fire detection or suppression and alarm systems • Uninterruptible power supply and alternate power generation equipment
1.3	Network hosting	The network and servers that supply client data to the offshore location should be hosted in a domestic U.S. location.
1.4	Data transmission	All data servers used to transmit data to or from an offshore location should use firewall technology that is satisfactory to the client. All client data either should be transmitted over private, vendor-owned data networks or, if public networks are used, should be protected and authenticated by cryptographic technology.
1.5	Cryptography	All data transmitted between the domestic and offshore locations should be encrypted. Connections using the Internet should be protected using a cryptographic technology that is approved by the client.
1.6	Data and information	Site policy should dictate that no client information may leave the worksite. The vendor should warrant that its policies, procedures, and systems comply with both U.S. and international data privacy laws. The vendor should use intrusion detection or prevention systems. The vendor should notify the client immediately of any event that may affect the security, availability, integrity, or confidentiality of the client's data.
1.7	Desktop	Desktop systems should not have hard drives, disk drives, or any operable ports accepting portable drives or media of any type that is capable of copying client information.
1.8	Audit	The client should have the right to audit the vendor's compliance with these requirements annually or if a security breach is suspected.

Table 21.1

Guidelines for Offshore Locations (Continued)

Number	Item	Guideline
2.0: Personnel and operations		
2.1	General	Only the site management team or personnel directly involved in providing services to the client should have access to the work area.
		All personnel servicing the client should have a separate area for storage of personal items.
2.2	Background checks	Background checks (including checks for criminal records, reference checks, and credit checks) and drug testing should be performed for all offshore employees before the vendor hires them.
2.3	Suspected terrorist screening	All offshore employees should be screened against the Terrorism Threat Integration Center master watch list or another international terrorism watch list approved by the client before the vendor hires them.
2.4	Training support	All personnel servicing the client should receive security and data privacy awareness training no less frequently than annually.
		To the extent that offshore resources require training from client personnel, the vendor will do one of the following:
		• Provide the client with videoconferencing facilities at no cost.
		• Pay for the travel expenses of client personnel traveling to the offshore location.
		• Have the offshore resources participate in training at a domestic U.S. location.
		The vendor should provide all training materials to the client for its review, upon request.
2.5	Turnover	The vendor should report to the client about turnover by position for all offshore personnel supporting the client no less frequently than on a semiannual basis. The vendor should address any concerns about excessive turnover to the client's satisfaction.
2.6	Holidays	The vendor should observe the same holidays in its offshore locations as at its domestic locations, except as otherwise approved by the client (i.e., the vendor should provide services on all non-U.S. holidays, regardless of holidays in the offshore location).
2.7	Availability	Any offshore employee who needs to contact client personnel for training or other purposes should be available during normal client business hours.
2.8	Subcontracting	Any subcontractors of incidental support services (e.g., security, cleaning) should also comply with these requirements.
		The vendor should audit and certify such subcontractors' compliance.

Table 21.1 continues

Table 21.1

Guidelines for Offshore Locations (Continued)

Number	Item	Guideline
3.0: Work rules		
3.1	General	Work rules at the vendor's offshore locations should be generally consistent with U.S. standards.
		The vendor should provide the client with a copy of its workplace policies and procedures upon request.
3.2	Employment requirements	The vendor should ensure that its employment requirements are consistent with certain U.S. standards, including
		• No forced or compulsory labor
		• No child labor
		• No discrimination
3.3	Work environment	The vendor should provide each offshore employee supplying services to the client a safe and healthy work environment, including a workspace no smaller than 6 feet by 6 feet.
3.4	Hours of work	The vendor should not require any offshore resources to work more than x hours per day, y days per week (or such lesser hours as may be required by local law).
3.5	Fair disciplinary practices	The vendor's policies should prohibit physical or mental punishment of employees.
3.6	Fair wages	The vendor should provide wages and benefits in compliance with local laws and at levels that address the basic needs of workers and their families.
3.7	Fair employment practices	The vendor should fulfill all of the legal and regulatory requirements of an employer in the country where services are being provided.
4.0: Change management		
4.1	Applications development	The vendor may use offshore resources for systems development and unit testing.
4.2	Requirements definition	The vendor may not use offshore resources for requirements definition that is related to change order.
4.3	Project management	The vendor should use domestic resources for project management activities.
4.4	Testing support	The vendor should ensure that its use of offshore resources does not change the client's access to or participation in acceptance testing.
4.5	Subcontracting	No services (except incidental services) provided offshore should be subcontracted without the client's express prior written consent.

Source: *Human Resources Outsourcing Forum—Offshoring Contract Guidelines,* April, 2005

PART VI

Hiring an Outsourcing
Consultant and Monitoring
Services and Trends

CHAPTER 22
Hiring a Consultant

Learning Why and When You May Need Help

This book provides more than 200 pages of guidance about how to evaluate and implement outsourcing arrangements. Yet it barely touches on the variety of issues that may arise in practice as an organization proceeds through the outsourcing journey. At the same time, many outsourcing decisions represent multimillion dollar purchasing decisions. Those circumstances—significant financial decisions made by staff members with limited experience—tend to suggest that most organizations would be better off engaging some experienced external help at various junctures during the process.

The typical outsourcing life cycle is illustrated in Figure 22.1. Each of the phases shown represents a natural point at which an external advisor's services might be useful. Some advisors specialize in specific phases, such as law firms specializing in contract negotiations, whereas other firms provide services across the entire outsourcing life cycle. For more complex outsourcing engagements, continuity throughout the entire process tends to be valuable and to reduce the overall cost of services, because the knowledge gained in the earlier phases can be leveraged during the later phases.

Figure 22.1
Outsourcing Life Cycle

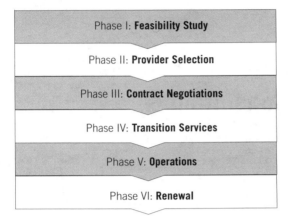

Phase I: **Feasibility Study**

Phase II: **Provider Selection**

Phase III: **Contract Negotiations**

Phase IV: **Transition Services**

Phase V: **Operations**

Phase VI: **Renewal**

Table 22.1 provides some guidance with respect to the circumstances under which external advisory support is most likely to be valuable, and it identifies some alternative approaches for situations in which your organization cannot necessarily afford as much external support as desired.

Finding Outsourcing Consultants

Given the size and rapid growth of the HR outsourcing marketplace, it is not surprising that a host of consulting firms offer some form of advisory services. There are four relatively distinct classes of consulting firms in the outsourcing industry:

International business process outsourcing advisory firms. These firms have their roots in information technology outsourcing services. Recently, the firms have expanded their consulting services to include various other types of BPO, including not only human resources but also finance, procurement, and other functions.

Traditional HR and benefit outsourcing advisory firms. These firms generally were established in the 1990s to support large companies seeking to outsource benefit administration. More recently, several of the firms have begun to expand their services to support the outsourcing of broader segments of HR, including even full-scale BPO of the entire function.

Table 22.1

External Assistance Alternatives

Phase	Full-Service Support Alternatives	Cost-Effective Alternatives
Feasibility study	Under this approach, the consultant manages the entire feasibility study process and uses its own tools and templates. This approach is appropriate if services are currently being performed internally and if the way the function will be performed will change significantly. An external advisor's assistance in building a comprehensive business case and in explaining the change management ramifications of outsourcing can be invaluable.	Feasibility studies can be performed using internal resources. Purchasing or procurement may be able to assist in developing the business case modeling. Another alternative is to work with a vendor to develop both the outsourcing service delivery model and the business case. The vendor is likely to be able to provide some context about change management that your internal resources will be lacking.
Provider selection	Under this approach, the consultant manages the entire vendor identification and selection process. This approach is usually appropriate when the services being outsourced represent expected annual vendor fees of $2 million or more. At that level, an external consultant is likely to pay for itself by managing an effective selection process; improving the definition of the services required; being familiar with market alternatives; and negotiating improved fees, service levels, or contract terms.	Some organizations elect to manage the vendor selection process and to use the external consultant as an advisor throughout the process.
Contract negotiations	Many organizations hire either a consultant or an external legal counsel to manage the contract negotiations process. This approach is appropriate if the outsourcing relationship is in a relatively immature industry or if the value of the contract exceeds $5 million over its term. An experienced advisor will be able to identify potential contractual pitfalls that may not be apparent.	Sometimes internal procurement or legal departments can manage the negotiations process and can use the services of the external advisor in a review capacity only.

Table 22.1 continues

Table 22.1

External Assistance Alternatives (Continued)

Phase	Full-Service Support Alternatives	Cost-Effective Alternatives
Transition services	Some organizations like to hire an external project manager or similar support resources to assist with the transition of services to the vendor. This approach is appropriate if the organization has limited resources available to support the transition.	There are individuals who specialize as independent project managers for large outsourcing projects. Your vendor or the external advisor who assisted your organization with vendor selection may be able to identify individuals for you to consider. Alternatively, some organizations retain the external advisor to provide over-the-shoulder consulting throughout the implementation process to ensure that the full scope of services is implemented and to provide experienced assistance in reviewing project and acceptance test plans.
Operations	Most HR organizations have experience managing a multitude of provider relationships. However, few of those existing relationships are as large and complex as some of the multifunction outsourcing projects that are now being established. For such organizations, it can make sense to hire an external consultant with expertise in vendor management on at least an interim basis until the necessary expertise has been developed internally.	More commonly, organizations hire external consultants to help them with specific tasks related to monitoring and managing their vendor relationships, such as benchmarking, monitoring service levels, or assisting in dispute resolution.

Table 22.1

External Assistance Alternatives (Continued)

Phase	Full-Service Support Alternatives	Cost-Effective Alternatives
Renewal	It is possible to hire an external consultant to manage the entire renewal process with an existing provider. This work would include both benchmarking the relationship and negotiating the renewal agreement.	The most valuable service that an external consultant can provide related to a renewal of an existing arrangement is to help calibrate the cost and quality of the existing relationship against current market alternatives. Prices in outsourcing can rise or fall, service enhancements can become new norms, and technological innovation can spawn new ways of performing the services. External consultants who are up to speed on current pricing, technology, and services can quickly help an organization assess how to revitalize an existing relationship for renewal, with the buyer taking the lead on the actual negotiations once the objectives have been established.

Other Large Full-Service Consulting firms. These firms are the international HR consulting firms like Mercer, Towers Perrin, and Watson Wyatt or the broad-based consulting firms like Deloitte or KMPG. The firms sometimes have teams that specialize in performing vendor selection processes and that have some level of expertise.

Small Professional Service Specialists. Outsourcing is generally recognized as a relatively specialized profession. Individuals who have participated in outsourcing engagements as part of either the purchaser or provider organization sometimes develop unique insights and experiences that can be translated into their own specialized consulting services. In some of the more mature areas of human resources, such as defined contribution administration, these small specialist organizations may offer a more cost-effective approach to securing some external assistance than the more traditional consulting approaches identified above.

Many other organizations also provide outsourcing assistance and guidance, albeit on a more limited scale and usually associated with some other context. For example, several large law firms tout their ability to get involved in the sourcing decision as early as the RFP process. Or management consulting firms that are helping clients design strategies for restructuring their firms may get involved in certain outsourcing vendor selections. But the majority of outsourcing consulting assistance is provided by one of the groups identified above.

Hiring the Right Consultant for Your Needs

The process of hiring the right consultant for your needs requires both an objective and a subjective set of filters. Although there are many different kinds of providers of outsourcing consulting assistance, a few factual circumstances surrounding each outsourcing engagement are likely to reduce the number of qualified consultants.

In the outsourcing consulting market, there are several key determinants of relative capability:

Depth of subject matter expertise. Many of the consultants who operate in this marketplace have expertise in outsourcing, but not all of them have expertise in HR subject matter. Although there are certainly common approaches for outsourcing different functional areas, working with a consultant who understands the HR function in some depth has its advantages.

Breadth of client experience. Perhaps not surprisingly, every client's needs are somewhat different. Although HR outsourcing services can be categorized into functional areas, there are significant variations from assignment to assignment. Ideally, your consultant will be familiar with a variety of clients, various vendor value strategies, and various outsourcing methods.

Vendor research and market data. Some parts of the HR outsourcing market are just emerging, and the vendors' capabilities are changing daily. It is a full-time job to keep track of the evolution of their service offerings. Clients should look for a consultant that is involved in research on a day-to-day basis to support its consulting services.

International capabilities. We would divide this category into two separate slices. In particular, international requirements for employees located in Canada and the United Kingdom are relatively common even among domestic HR assignments. So the need for international capabilities within your advisory firm is more important when your requirements include services outside those countries. Also, there are differences in the levels of awareness and understanding of the vendors' offshoring and near-shoring locations that may apply even for domestic services, so this is an area that clients may want to explore carefully with potential advisors.

Scope of the assignment. The potential value of the outsourcing engagement should be consistent with the fees for the consulting services. If you just want help managing the RFP process itself but are relatively confident with the function being outsourced, you may find it appropriate to hire a different kind of organization than you would for a global outsourcing engagement covering many new and emerging outsourcing topics.

Even with these filters, it is easy to become overwhelmed with the prospect of identifying the right consultant for your project. However, once you have identified the general classification of consulting firms that seems appropriate for your needs, you can refer to a couple of good sources of information to help you reduce the list of consultants under consideration. Perhaps the easiest way to begin to winnow the list is to contact your peers in human resources at other companies. Most organizations today have had multiple experiences with outsourcing various segments of human resources. A few well-placed calls to your peers are likely to produce a relatively short list of consultants with whom they have had success in the past.

Interestingly, one of the best sources for potential consultants is the vendor community itself. Although it is likely that vendors will recommend consultants from whom they have had success winning business in the past, they are also much more likely to recommend consultants who (a) have experience with similar situations, (b) have earned the respect of the vendor community as a purveyor of consulting services, and (c) have satisfied clients. After all, vendors will already be competing for your business by trying to provide you with useful information that will confirm their knowledge of the industry.

Examining a Sample Consulting Contract

Historically, many organizations were relatively lackadaisical about codifying their consulting relationships. Consultants performed the services requested by their clients on a fee-for-service basis, and clients relied on their professional advice. However, as the use of consultants has increased, most companies have migrated toward establishing more formal relationships with their external advisors. Today, it is generally recognized as a best practice that most consulting services should be performed under some type of contractual agreement.

The simplest and most flexible approach to contracting for consulting services is to establish a master consulting agreement and then to purchase consulting services on a project-by-project basis. For each assignment, the consultant is asked to draft a scope of services document that describes the services to be performed, the staff members who will work on the project, the expected duration of the project, and the cost of the assignment. The consultant's fees may be based on either a fee-for-service approach or a fixed-fee approach. In practice, a fee-for-service approach combined with a not-to-exceed limit may offer the best possible arrangement for the buyer of services. The accompanying CD-ROM provides an example of a very simple consulting services agreement that can serve as the master agreement for a variety of consulting arrangements.

CHAPTER 23

Seeing Trends and the Future of Outsourcing

Learning What Lies Ahead

Today, outsourcing is a major trend that is flowing across the landscape of American business and changing the way that corporations are organized and create value. As we have seen throughout this book, HR is not immune to such changes. Instead, outsourcing is rapidly becoming the preferred strategy for more organizations with respect to the delivery components of the HR function.

And outsourcing as a strategy is not limited to human resources. Instead, it is being used to transform the American corporation in ways not previously envisioned. The exact form of the typical large organization once this transformation is complete is not yet possible to define. But it appears (a) that organizations will be much more focused on a few core strategic values, such as research, product design, or marketing, and (b) that specialist organizations will be engaged on an outsourced basis to perform various aspects of operating the company and supporting employees.

As in the case of any major trend, excesses in the use of outsourcing will no doubt occur. Some companies will find that they have inadvertently outsourced functions that were core to their value propositions and that should have remained an internal activity. Many HR professionals ask themselves if outsourcing in their area is a fad that may one day reverse itself. We think it unlikely that HR outsourcing is a fad given the specifics of today's marketplace. In particular, HR is a more homogeneous function than many of its counterparts such as IT, finance, manufacturing, or procurement. All organizations must perform most HR delivery functions. They must attract, hire, pay, evaluate, and promote employees. Such fundamental processes tend to be inherently similar, with the variations limited to the manner in which companies communicate with their employees.

HR lends itself to a reasonable level of replication and consistency. And there already exists a community of vendors that are making investments to develop the solutions that organizations desire. Unlike any one organization that must make such investment decisions on the basis of its own return on investment profile, vendors have an entirely different value proposition. Outsourcing vendors may choose to invest in areas such as performance management or talent development merely to create a competitive advantage that allows them to acquire more business. The potential size of the outsourcing market for HR services, estimated to exceed $100 billion by both Gartner and IDS, is likely to encourage investment in systems and capabilities that have never before made sense. As those investments take root and new capabilities to perform value-added HR functions are made available, the rush to outsourcing is likely to accelerate, not diminish.

So we expect that most HR delivery functions, such as workforce administration, payroll, recruiting, compensation, and learning, will follow in the footsteps of the various benefit administration functions that were outsourced in the 1990s. And what organization today would even think of bringing back in house defined contribution or defined benefit administration? Few case studies in the history of those outsourcing markets suggest that the pendulum may swing back. Using history as a guide, we would suggest that the outsourcing of human resources is here to stay.

Anticipating Trends

Therefore, HR professionals should anticipate an inexorable trend toward more outsourcing in human resources. The question is no longer whether most large organizations will outsource most of their HR function, but rather when they will do so.

Figure 23.1 summarizes the current use of outsourcing solutions among large organizations.

Figure 23.1
Use of Outsourcing by Functional Area

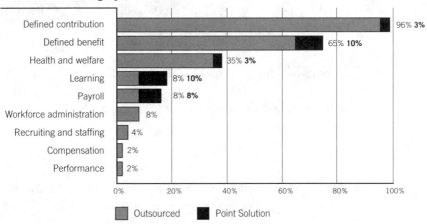

Source: Gildner & Associates Prevalence Database ™ for large employers (those with more than 10,000 employees)

Using this chart as a starting point, we would anticipate the following trends to sweep through human resources over the next decade.

- More than 30 percent of large organizations will have adopted outsourcing for their workforce administration function by the year 2010, and that percentage will continue to grow thereafter.

- Most organizations will migrate to a vendor's proprietary HRIS system at about the same time, thereby marking the slow demise of the current dominance by the software application providers.

- Responsibility for payroll administration will increasingly be transferred back to human resources from finance and will be outsourced in conjunction with workforce administration.

- There will be a rapid adoption of the use of outsourcing for fulfilling most nonexempt and clerical job positions, closely following the migration to outsourced workforce administration.

- New approaches to talent development, including integrated performance management and learning administration, will be spawned and will ultimately become one of the competitive differentiators among broad-based HR vendors.

- The vendor community will deliver real-time workforce analytics that have never been available before, which will significantly enhance the ability of internal Centers of Excellence to monitor their function and to fulfill their lofty names.

- An increasing percentage of HR delivery transactional activity will be performed in off-shore locations such as India, Malaysia, and China, thus driving down the cost of HR on a per-employee basis.

- Local language support for global populations will become increasingly available as the vendors introduce their global HR transactional capabilities, which are contained in their new proprietary platforms.

- Human resources will become a leader among the corporate administrative functions as it is being positioned to provide a global scalable infrastructure around the world; HR will also be marked by declining unit costs over the next two decades.

Those trends, which can all be observed today in their nascent stages, suggest a dynamic environment for HR over the next twenty years. HR professionals who grasp the significance of the impending transformation of the function should be able to enjoy unparalleled career opportunities and challenges. It is hoped that your preparation for this transformation within human resources has been enhanced by reading this book.

Appendix: Abbreviations and Acronyms

Abbreviations and acronyms are handy because they allow us to quickly express long terms. The following list provides many of the abbreviations and acronyms in use in HR management. These abbreviations will be helpful as outsource HR activities.

AAA	American Arbitration Association
AAI	ASPA Accreditation Institute
AAP	Affirmative Action Program
ABO	Accumulated benefit obligation
ACA	American Compensation Association
ACLU	American Civil Liberties Union
ACP	Actual compensation percentage
AD&D	Accidental death and dismemberment
ADA	Americans with Disabilities Act of 1990
ADEA	Age Discrimination in Employment Act of 1967
ADP	Actual deferral percentage
AFL-CIO	American Federation of Labor and Congress ofIndustrial Organizations
AFSCME	American Federation of State, County, and Municipal Employees
AICC	Aviation Industry Computer-Based Training Committee
ANSI	American National Standards Institute
APL	Accreditation of prior learning
APPWP	Association of Private Pension and Welfare Plans
ASO	Administrative services only (contract)
ASP	Application service provider
ASPA	American Society of Pension Actuaries; also stands for American Society for Personnel Administrators, the former name of the Society for Human Resource Management (SHRM)
ASTD	American Society for Training and Development
BFOQ	Bona fide occupational qualification
BLS	Bureau of Labor Statistics (Department of Labor)
BPO	Business process outsourcing
BNA	Bureau of National Affairs
CAD	Computer-aided design
CAI	Computer-assisted instruction
CAM	Computer-aided manufacturing
CCP	Certified compensation professional
CCPA	Council of Canadian Personnel Associations
CDN	Content delivery network
CEB	Council on Employee Benefits
CEBS	Certified employee benefits specialist
CFR	Code of Federal Regulations

CFR	Code of Federal Regulations
COB	Coordination of benefits
COBRA	Consolidated Omnibus Budget Reconciliation Act of 1985
CODA	Cash or deferred plan or arrangement
COL	Cost of living
COLA	Cost-of-living adjustment
COLI	Corporate-owned life insurance
CPI	Consumer price index
CUPA	College and University Personnel Association
D&B	Dun & Bradstreet
D&O	Directors and officers (liability insurance)
DA	Deposit administration
DEFRA	Deficit Reduction Act of 1984
DHHS	Department of Health and Human Services (formerly the Department of Health, Education, and Welfare, or HEW; see also HHS)
DOL	Department of Labor
EAP	Employee assistance program
EBRI	Employee Benefit Research Institute
EBSA	Employee Benefits Security Administration (Department of Labor; formerly the Pension and Welfare Benefits Administration, or PWBA)
ECFC	Employer's Council of Flexible Compensation
EEO	Equal employment opportunity
EEOC	Equal Employment Opportunity Commission
EFT	Electronic funds transfer
EPO	Exclusive provider organization
ER	Employee relations
ERIC	ERISA Industry Committee
ERISA	Employee Retirement Income Security Act of 1974
ERTA	Economic Recovery Tax Act of 1981
ESA	Employment Standards Administration (Department of Labor)
ESOP	Employee stock ownership plan
ETA	Employment and Training Administration (Department of Labor)
FASB	Financial Accounting Standards Board
FCRA	Fair Credit Reporting Act of 1970
FDA	Food and Drug Administration (Department of Health and Human Services)
FEP	Fair employment practice
FEPCA	Federal Employees Pay Comparability Act of 1990
FERF	Financial Executives Research Foundation
FICA	Federal Insurance Contributions Act of 1937
FLRA	Federal Labor Relations Authority
FLSA	Fair Labor Standards Act of 1938
FMLA	Family and Medical Leave Act of 1993
FPCA	Federal Pay Comparability Act of 1970

FSA	Flexible spending account
FTC	Federal Trade Commission (Department of Commerce)
FTE	Full-time equivalent
FUTA	Federal Unemployment Tax Act of 1939
GIC	Guaranteed investment contract; also stands for guaranteed interest contract
GLSO	Group Legal Services Organization
GOC	General occupational classification
GSA	General Services Administration
GULP	Group universal life program
HHS	Department of Health and Human Services (see also DHHS)
HIAA	Health Insurance Association of America
HIPAA	Health Insurance Portability and Accountability Act of 1996
HMO	Health maintenance organization
HMOA	Health Maintenance Organization Act of 1973
HR	Human resources
HRIS	Human resource information system
HRMS	Human resource management system
HRO	Human resource outsourcing
HUD	Department of Housing and Urban Development
IABC	International Association of Business Communicators
IAPES	International Association of Personnel in Employment Security
IFEBP	International Foundation of Employee Benefit Plans
IHF	Industrial Health Foundation
ILR	Industrial and labor relations
ILT	Instructor-led training
IPA	Individual Practice Association
IPG	Immediate participation guarantee
IPMA	International Personnel Management Association
IR	Industrial relations
IRA	Individual retirement account
IRC	Internal Revenue Code
IRCA	Immigration Reform and Control Act of 1986
IRRA	Industrial Relations Research Association
IRS	Internal Revenue Service (Department of the Treasury)
ISO	Incentive stock option
IT	Information technology
JTPA	Job Training Partnership Act of 1982
KPI	Key performance indicator
KSAs	Knowledge, skills, and abilities
LCMS	Learning content management system
LMRA	Labor Management Relations Act of 1947 (also called the Taft-Hartley Act)
LMRDA	Labor-Management Reporting and Disclosure Act of 1959
LMS	Learning management system

LTD	Long-term disability
MFBE	Minority/female business enterprise
NCPE	National Committee on Pay Equity
NIC	National Industrial Council
NIOSH	National Institute for Occupational Safety and Health (Centers for Disease Control and Prevention)
NLRA	National Labor Relations Act of 1935
NLRB	National Labor Relations Board
NPA	Negotiated provider agreement
NQSO	Nonqualified stock option
OAS	Old-Age Security Act of 1952 (Canada)
OASDHI	Old-age, survivors, disability, and hospital insurance
OASDI	Old-age, survivors, and disability insurance
OBRA	Omnibus Budget Reconciliation Act (annual act)
OFCCP	Office of Federal Contract Compliance Programs (Department of Labor)
OJT	On-the-job training
OMB	Office of Management and Budget
OPM	Office of Personnel Management
OSH	Occupational Safety and Health (Act of 1970)
OSHA	Occupational Safety and Health Administration; also may refer to the Occupational Safety and Health Act of 1970
OSHRC	Occupational Safety and Health Review Commission
OWERP	Open window early retirement plans
OWBPA	Older Workers Benefit Protection Act of 1990
PAYSOP	Payroll-based employee stock ownership plan
PBGC	Pension Benefit Guarantee Corporation
PCP	Primary care physician
PDA	Pregnancy Discrimination Act of 1978
PIA	Primary insurance amount (social security)
PPA	Pension Protection Act of 2005
PPI	Producer price index
PPO	Preferred provider organization
PSRO	Professional Standards Review Organization
QA	Quality assurance
QC	Quality control
QDRO	Qualified domestic relations order
QJSA	Qualified joint and survivor annuity
QMCSO	Qualified medical child support order
QPSA	Qualified pre-retirement survivor annuity
R&C	Reasonable and customary
REA	Retirement Equity Act of 1984
RFI	Request for information
RFP	Request for proposal

RIF	Reduction in force
RTK	Right to know
S&P	Standard & Poor's
SAR	Summary annual report; also can refer to stock appreciation right
SAS	Statement on Auditing Standards
SBA	Small Business Administration
SEC	Securities and Exchange Commission
SEP	Simplified employee pension
SERP	Supplemental executive retirement plan
SHRM	Society for Human Resource Management
SLA	Service level agreement
SOX	Sarbanes-Oxley Act
SOXLEY	Sarbanes-Oxley Act
SPD	Summary plan description (benefits)
SSA	Social Security Act of 1935; also may refer to the Social Security Administration
STD	Short-term disability
SUB	Supplemental unemployment benefit
TAMRA	Technical and Miscellaneous Revenue Act of 1988
TBO	Total benefits outsourcing
TEFRA	Tax Equity and Fiscal Responsibility Act of 1982
T-H	Taft-Hartley (Act of 1947; also called the Labor Management Relations Act)
TJTC	Targeted jobs tax credit
TPA	Third-party administrator
TPRA	Taxpayer Relief Act of 1997
TRA	Tax Reform Act (various years)
TRASOP	Tax Reduction Act (employee) stock ownership plan
TSA	Tax-sheltered annuity
TUPE	Transfer of Undertakings (Protection of Employment) (Regulations)
UC	Unemployment compensation
UR	Utilization review
USERRA	Uniformed Services Employment and Reemployment Rights Act of 1994
VEBA	Voluntary employees' beneficiary association (also known as a 501(c)(9) trust)
W&S	Wage and salary
WBT	Web-based training
WC	Workers' compensation
WOTC	Work opportunity tax credit

Index

W

About the Authors

Mary F. Cook is the founding partner of Mary Cook & Associates, a human resource consulting firm based in Scottsdale, Arizona. Ms. Cook has many years of experience as an HR generalist and consultant. She has written more than a dozen books on HR management and is an international lecturer on that topic. Her books are published in several languages around the world. You may reach Ms. Cook at marycook2@cox.net.

Scott B. Gildner is the global HR practice leader for TPI, a leading sourcing advisory firm. Before joining TPI, he was founder and president of Gildner & Associates, an HR outsourcing advisory firm in the United States, also headquartered in Scottsdale, Arizona. Mr. Gildner has more than 25 years of experience as an actuary, outsourcing service provider executive, and outsourcing consultant. He is a frequent contributor to the outsourcing media and a nationally recognized authority on outsourcing in human resources. He has assisted more than 70 Fortune 500 organizations with developing and implementing their strategies for outsourcing various HR functions. You can reach Mr. Gildner at scott.gildner@tpi.net.

Other Books from SHRM

Selected Additional Titles from the Society for Human Resource Management (SHRM®)

Building Profit through Building People
> By Ken Carrig and Patrick M. Wright

Diverse Teams at Work
> By Lee Gardenswartz and Anita Rowe

The Future of Human Resources Management
Editors David Ulrich, Mike Losey, and Sue Meisinger

HR Source Book Series
Performance Appraisal Source Book
> By Mike Deblieux

HIPAA Privacy Source Book

> By William S. Hubbartt, SPHR, CCP

Hiring Source Book

> By Cathy Fyock, CAP, SPHR

Trainer's Diversity Source Book
> By Jonamay Lambert, M.A. and Selma Myers, M.A.

Harvard/SHRM Series on Business Literacy for HR Professionals
> Series Advisor Wendy Bliss, J.D., SPHR

Essentials of Finance and Budgeting
Essentials of Managing Change and Transition
Essentials of Negotiation

Human Resource Essentials: Your Guide to Starting and Running the HR Function
> By Lin Grensing-Pophal, SPHR

Manager of Choice: 5 Competencies for Cultivating Top Talent
> By Nancy S. Ahlrichs

Managing Employee Retention: A Strategic Accountability Approach
> By Jack J. Phillips, Ph.D. and Adele O. Connell, Ph.D.

Practical HR Series

Legal, Effective References: How to Give and Get Them
By Wendy Bliss, J.D., SPHR

Investigating Workplace Harassment: How to Be Fair, Thorough, and Legal
By Amy Oppenheimer, J.D., and Craig Pratt, MSW, SPHR

Proving the Value of HR: How and Why to Measure ROI
By Jack J. Phillips, Ph.D. and Patricia Pulliam Phillips, Ph.D.

Responsible Restructuring: Creative and Profitable Alternatives to Layoffs
By Wayne F. Cascio

Retaining Your Best Employees (In Action Case Studies)
Series Editor Jack J. Phillips

Supervisor's Guide to Labor Relations
By T.O. Collier, Jr.

Understanding the Federal Wage & Hour Laws: What Employers Must Know about FLSA and its Overtime Regulations
By Seyfarth Shaw LLP

TO ORDER SHRM BOOKS

SHRM offers a member discount on all books that it publishes or sells. To order this or any other book published by the Society, contact the SHRMStore.®

ONLINE: www.shrm.org/shrmstore
BY PHONE: 800-444-5006 (option #1); or
770-442-8633 (ext. 362); or TDD 703-548-6999
BY FAX: 770-442-9742
BY MAIL: SHRM Distribution Center
P.O. Box 930132
Atlanta, GA 31193-0132
USA

Using the Accompanying CD-ROM

The materials on the accompanying CD-Rom are readable on a PC and are in two formats: Portable Document Format (PDF) and Rich Text Format (RTF).

Portable Document Format (PDF) Files

To open the PDF files, all you need is the free Adobe® Reader®. The PDF files on this disc are compatible with Reader versions 5.0.0 and higher. Adobe Reader or the full version of Acrobat is required. You can download the latest version of Adobe Reader for free at http://www.adobe.com/products/acrobat/readstep2.html. See also the section "Getting Started," below.

Rich Text Form (RTF) Files

The RTF files can be opened in many word-processing programs. You will be given the option to download these files. See "Getting Started," below. **NOTE: The RTF files are "read only." To adapt them for your use, open a file and safe it under a different name. You will be able to edit that new file.**

Getting Started

To access the files on the CD-ROM, insert the CD-ROM into your compact disk drive. The disk will AutoRun and open a preliminary screen; click "Next" to proceed. You will see an information screen "Using the Accompanying CD-ROM;" click "Next." The disk will give you the option to either open the PDF files or install the RTF files. If you select the PDF files, the disk will either open those files OR will tell you that you need to get Adobe Reader. Follow the directions on your screen.

The CD-ROM accompanying this book contains additional materials to help you in your outsourcing project. There is a list of often-used acronyms, a complete glossary of HR and outsourcing terms, and sample materials and agreements that will prevent you from re-inventing the outsourcing wheel.

STOP!

Please read the following before opening the CD-ROM accompanying this book.

By opening the CD-ROM package, you are agreeing to be bound by the following agreement:

Once you open the seal on the software package, this book and the CD-ROM are nonrefundable. (With the seal unbroken, the book and CD-ROM are refundable only under the terms generally allowed by the seller.)

This software product is protected by copyright and all rights are reserved by the Society for Human Resource Management (SHRM®) and its licensors. Purchasers of the book may use the materials on the CD-ROM as part of their own work providing that that include the full crediting.

Copying the software to another medium or format for use on a single computer is permitted and therefore does not violate the U.S. Copyright Law. Copying the software for any other purposes is not permitted and is therefore a violation of the U.S. Copyright Law.

This software product is sold as is without warranty of an kind, either express or implied, including but not limited to the implied warranty of merchantability and fitness for a particular purpose. Neither SHRM more its dealers or distributors assumes any liability for any alleged or actual damage arising from the use of or the inability to use this software. (Some states to now allow the exclusion of implied warranties, so the exclusion may not apply to you if you receive this product in such a state.)

CD-ROM Contents

Abbreviations and Acronyms Used in HR Outsourcing
Glossary of Human Resource and Outsourcing Terms
Sample Request for Information (RIF)
Sample Overview to a Request for Proposals (RFP)
Sample Administrative Services Agreement
Sample Consulting Services Agreement